Fundamentals
of Effective
Group Communication

Fundamentals of Effective Group Communication

Carl L. Kell
Western Kentucky University

Paul R. Corts
Oklahoma Baptist University

Macmillan Publishing Co., Inc.
New York

Collier Macmillan Publishers
London

To Mary Anne and Diane

Copyright © 1980, Macmillan Publishing Co., Inc.
Printed in the United States of America

All rights reserved. No part of this book may be reproduced or transmitted in any form or by any means, electronic or mechanical, including photocopying, recording, or any information storage and retrieval system, without permission in writing from the Publisher.

Macmillan Publishing Co., Inc.
866 Third Avenue, New York, New York 10022

Collier Macmillan Canada, Ltd.

Library of Congress Cataloging in Publication Data

Kell, Carl L
    Fundamentals of effective group communication.

    Bibliography: p.
    Includes index.
    1. Communication in small groups. 2. Decision-making, Group. I. Corts, Paul R., joint author. II. Title.
HM133.K43 1980   301.18'5   79-15877
ISBN 0-02-362280-6

Printing: 1 2 3 4 5 6 7 8   Year: 0 1 2 3 4 5 6

Preface

If "talking" could solve the ills of our society, we would have been done with those problems long ago. Mere words don't "cut the mustard" in these days of social activism, or everyday discussion situations.

Our attempts to help you achieve productive discussion behaviors are motivated by our deep-seated belief that only the acquisition of skills in communication can adequately and satisfactorily solve the problems encountered by small groups. Moreover, we believe firmly in the prevailing argument for *communication competency,* and for the metaphorical concept of the *maturing* group member and *mature* small group.

No one in the speech communication field, as of this writing, has developed a test or series of tests to assess communication competence. Nevertheless, in the effort to provide guidelines in group-centered communication competencies, we have drawn boldly, with a sense of the sheer madness in the venture, on the research literature in small group communication for suggestion and direction. We hope that you, together with your instructor, can come to grips with the basics of small-group communication, your role as a contributing member of your group, the behaviors that you should blend into your communication, and the behaviors that you should avoid in your communication.

We acknowledge the major contributors to this text: the semester-upon-semester classes of students by whom we have been taught and with whom we probably have shared precious little in substance and instructional support. We have truly been the learner in all of our combined years of instruction. We are also indebted to our colleagues at home and across the country for their support and review of our efforts. We are especially indebted to Jo Anne Graham, Bronx Community College, Bronx, N.Y., and William E. Jurma, University of Michigan, Ann Arbor, for their thoughtful and constructive reviews of *Fundamentals of Effective Group Communication* during its preparation.

In the future, in the present, the person trained in small-group skills will be a valued employee in the public and private sector of our economy, for futurist scholars have stated that by the year 2000, half of the jobs in our country will be *service*-related. That astonishing prediction means that there will likely be a high priority in hiring and firing practices for people trained in effective interpersonal and problem-solving communication skills. Need we say more?

Yes, there is one more thing. We believe firmly that training in small group communication behaviors can help you become a more well-rounded human being. *Fundamentals of Effective Group Communication* is predicated on an accepted tradition of speech communication, that of "showing you better visions of your *self* and the ways to get along with your fellow human beings."

We wish you every success with your experiences in small group communication situations and we hope that even your failures will provide opportunities for learning and growth. We also wish for you the joy of a shared activity done well, enhanced by the expectations of continued success in the enterprise of communication essential to all human relationships.

CARL L. KELL
PAUL R. CORTS

Contents

1
**The Nature of Small-Group
Communication: Types and Formats**   1
  Objectives 1
  Uses of Small-Group Communication 4
  Small-Group Communication As Process 6
  Purposes for Small-Group Communication 9
  Fact Finding 10
  Information Sharing 11
  Decision Making 13
  Formats for Small-Group Communication 17
  When to Use Small-Group Communication 21
  Summary 26
  References and Further Reading 26

2
Preparation for Group Discussion   29
  Objectives 29
  The Initial Planning: Who, What, Why, When, Where 32
  Preparation for Presentation 43
  Summary 54
  References and Further Reading 55

3
**Psychological Aspects
of Group Communication**   57
  Objectives 57
  What Makes You Tick 60

Why Join a Group? 63
Psychological Characteristics in Group Discussion 63
Okay, Where Do We Go From Here? 68
Summary 69
References and Further Reading 70

4
The Nature of Interpersonal and Group Communication: A Competency Approach — 73
Objectives 73
Interpersonal Communication Competencies 76
Small Group Communication Competencies 78
Techniques Test 82
Phases in Integrated Problem Solving (PIPS) 89
Summary 100
References and Further Reading 100

5
Nonverbal Dimensions of Group Discussion — 103
Objectives 103
Nonverbal Communication Systems 110
Observing and Interpreting Nonverbal Communication 118
Test Your Nonverbal Reading Ability 121
Summary 146
References and Further Reading 151

6
Leadership—Followership: A Competency Approach — 153
Objectives 153
Leadership Characteristics Worksheet 155

Leadership—Followership Expectations 158
Leadership and Group Performance 159
Leadership Characteristics—A Simulated Problem-
  Solving Experience 161
Summary 164
References and Further Reading 165

7
Evaluation/Assessment Systems for Group Communication 167
Objectives 167
Formative/Summative Evaluation 169
Evaluating the Individual Participant 170
Summary 182
References and Further Reading 183

8
When Groups Go Good or Bad: Effective Strategies 185
Objectives 185
When "Groups Go Good" 187
When "Groups Go Bad" 190
Characteristics of a Functioning Mature Group 193
Summary 194
References and Further Reading 194

Index 197

The Nature of Small-Group Communication: Types and Formats

OBJECTIVES:
After studying this chapter, you should be better able to:

Define small-group communication.

Understand the uses of small-group communication in everyday living, in the business/professional world, and in social/cultural life.

Identify and describe the basic types of small-group communication.

Identify and describe the basic formats of small-group communication.

Appreciate small-group communication as a useful process for fact finding, information sharing, and decision making.

Judge situations in which the use of small-group communication is most appropriate.

Appreciate the strengths and weaknesses of small-group communication.

FUNDAMENTALS OF GROUP COMMUNICATION[1]

GENERAL KNOWLEDGE ABOUT GROUP COMMUNICATION	TASK DIMENSION	SOCIAL DIMENSION	ASSESSMENT
1. **Nature/Usefulness** 2. **Types/Format** 3. **The Process and Its Phases** 4. **Strengths/Weaknesses**	1. Planning/Preparation 2. Procedures/Arrangements 3. Interpersonal/Group Communication Competencies 4. Phases of Integrated Problem Solving 5. Leadership Responsibilities	1. Self/Group Characteristics 2. Self/Group Concepts 3. Interpersonal/Group Attraction 4. Social Attributes 5. Dimensions of Nonverbal Behavior 6. Leadership Characteristics 7. Role/Status/Power 8. Mature/Immature Group Characteristics	1. Formative/Summative 2. Individual/Group Evaluation Technique 3. Maturing Member/Group: Strengths and Weaknesses

[1]Concepts in bold face are emphasized in this chapter.

Small-group communication occurs when a small group cooperatively interacts through purposeful communication. This definition makes it clear that three main components will effect small-group communication: (1) *a small group*, (2) *cooperative interaction through communication*, and (3) *a purpose*.

"What is a small group?" you may ask. In the context of group communication, a small group is one that normally numbers from two to approximately eight people. Obviously the small group requires a minimum of two participants. One of the formats that will be discussed later in this chapter is called dialogue and involves two primary participants. Informally, you probably frequently discuss in dyads, or two-person units. For example, should you and a friend be discussing an upcoming test in chemistry so that you can determine the best way to study for the exam, the two of you are engaging in small-group communication. You number at least two people; you are cooperatively interacting through communication; and you have a purpose: preparing for the test in chemistry.

There is, however, a limit to the number that can be included in a group and still be referred to as a small group. In the context of this book we will consider eight to ten participants as the maximum small group and a group of five to seven as the optimum (Bormann, 1975).

As our definition indicates, *cooperative interaction through communication* is desirable. If the small group is not cooperating, other terms such as "debate" or "argument" would more appropriately characterize the interaction. Positive interpersonal relationships are essential for effective small-group communication; at least one writer views interaction as a synonymous term for small-group communication (Shaw, 1976). Interaction also involves participation, participation by all of those who are a part of the group. The essence of communication may occur orally or nonverbally but communicative intent is necessary.

The third element of our definition is *purpose*. Barnlund (1968) describes the need for "focused" interaction. This implies the desire or hope to achieve an end. Although the purpose for small-group communication has usually been stated and made known to members of the group, it can sometimes be motivated by hidden reasons, too. The basic purposes for small-group communication with which we will be concerned in this text are fact finding, information sharing, and decision making. True, these purposes are all closely interrelated, but to facilitate explanation we will separate them from time to time.

Uses of Small-Group Communication

The average citizen uses small-group communication in a tremendous variety of ways in everyday living. Miller (1966) suggests that some critics of our society believe we are "hyper-organized"; others contend we must maintain our group organizations to preserve our American freedom traditions.

A large portion of the working day of the average person employed in business and industry is spent in some type of small-group communication. Many executives will spend this time in more or less formal meetings. Others employed in business and industry will spend this time in conversations with fellow workers, supervisors, or subordinates. What is true for those employed in business and industry is also true for those of us who walk other avenues of life. If you will reflect on your own use of time over the past few days or weeks, you will discover that a significant amount of it was spent in small-group communication.

Consider relationships in the home. Child-to-child and child-to-parent communication predominated in the home as you grew up, a setting in which the informal use of small-group communication prevails for a large percentage of the time; at least some of this communication surely would qualify for description as small-group communication.

The Nature of Small-Group Communication

In the college days you are experiencing right now, there are a variety of opportunities for small-group discussion. These include the informal settings of dormitory "bull sessions," the "chit-chat" in the cafeteria, or the "rapping" that might develop in the student center. There are, of course, many opportunities for more formalized discussion, too—in settings such as student government meetings, fraternity/sorority meetings, dormitory organizations, clubs, honor organizations, and probably even in some classrooms!

In the years following your graduation, you will find many opportunities for group discussion in your business/professional life. Large businesses and industrial giant corporations, for example, frequently use executive leadership groups for key decision making. This process is in sharp contrast to the days of old when one man frequently operated as *the* decision maker. Business, industry, and the professions also rely on many committees or task forces to engage in problem-solving activities.

When a problem occurs in preparation for a rocket launch or space flight, a team of experts works together to analyze the problem and arrive at the best solution. A number of doctors are usually called in when there is a patient with a special or critical problem. The group of doctors reviews the situation and collectively makes a judgment. Industrial product development utilizes a team approach with a head project engineer working with a large staff of product research and design personnel. In all of these examples, the group or team approach is used and small-group communcation plays a key role in each.

There are other professional occupations such as law, labor relations, and public diplomacy that require critical teamwork efforts and rely heavily on the small-group communication process. Our entire government system, which honors government *of* the people and *by* the people, necessitates the strong involvement of many people. These many voices operate through deliberative bodies such as a house of representatives, a senate, a city council, a city commission, a Supreme Court, and the like. These deliberative bodies utilize small-group communication on a formal and informal basis to shape the opinions of many into a single voice of decision. This is the American participatory government system.

In like manner, much of our social and community life follows a similar pattern. We have groups such as the Parent–Teacher Associations (PTA), Republican and Democratic Party organizations, the YWCA/YWCA, our churches and synagogues, and many others. These kinds of organizations usually have large meetings that function formally according to parliamentary procedure, but they also contain many small subgroups. There is, therefore, abundant small-group communication evolving from participation in these types of organizations. And most of us are members of many other less formal groups, including literary clubs, sewing circles, sports clubs, neighborhood groups, and a host of others—all of which depend considerably on small-group communication.

Some groups that make strict use of informal small-group communication will not be specifically dealt with in this text. Some of the organizations mentioned are highly structured and very formal. This text is concerned with the more formalized types of small-group communication that operate in a variety of spheres, including the field of education, business, industry, civic/professional organizations, churches, government, and others. Formalized small-group communication follows certain patterns and has certain organizational elements to it that define its domain much more clearly than is the case with informal small-group communication. Definitions, rules, standard procedures, and similar material create a body of knowledge concerning formalized small-group communication. This text is devoted primarily to the formal type. Hopefully, it offers much of significance for use in informal and less structured small-group situations.

Small-Group Communication as Process

Communicating in a small group does not just happen; it develops. Communication itself is viewed as a process with a sequential pattern of development. Tubbs (1978) conceptualizes small-group interaction in the format of a "systems" approach.

The Nature of Small-Group Communication

Whether small-group communication is described as a system or a process, there is order and interrelatedness to its parts. To say that small-group communication is a process means that various steps or stages lead in a reasonably predictable pattern toward an end.

Figure 1-1 shows a simple five-step communication model. Communication follows a predictable pattern of a source that originates the communication message, which then must be encoded into some form for transmission through some type of channel. The decoder receives the message from the channel and interprets the message to the final destination. In human oral communication, the process flows from message creation in a person's mind (source) into appropriate language and speed (encoder), which flows through airwaves (channel) to the communicative recipient who hears the speech and interprets the language meaning (decoder). Finally, the message reaches the mind of the recipient (destination).

In the communication process the general thrust is forward, and the repetition of this process enables a person to anticipate what is to come through a *feed forward* process. As the destination element of the process communicates back to the source, the source obtains a reaction to consider in making future communication. The process of the destination communicating back to the source is known as *feedback*.

The information and impressions gained through the feed forward and feedback processes are extremely helpful to us in communicating. For example, a person (source) may be communicating to another (destination) and the listener (destination) may interrupt the source by saying something such as, "I know exactly what you're trying to say." The listener (destination) assumed a conclusion before it had been fully articulated

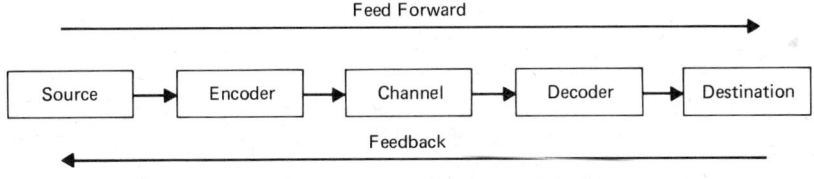

Figure 1-1. Communication Model.

by the speaker (source) because prior experience (feed forward) had caused the listener (destination) to anticipate.

Feedback occurs in many communication situations. As we speak, we often shape our continued comments on the basis of the reactions generated by our earlier comments. These reactions may be nonverbal responses from listeners such as a frown or smile, or they may be verbal comments. For example, a speaker (source) says to another (destination), "I really believe we ought to do this." The listener says, "It sounds great to me." In this case, the speaker obtains positive feedback and feels comfortable proceeding. If, on the other hand, the listener had said, "I think it would cause some serious problems," the speaker obtains cautious feedback that will probably evoke additional discussion. Or, the speaker might have received negative feedback, such as, "I completely disagree." In any case, the feedback would be evaluated by the speaker before he or she determines how to proceed.

Communication occurs only through some form of process. The source cannot communicate directly to the destination without intervening process elements occurring.

In small-group communication, there are two process dimensions that will receive emphasis in this text, the task and the social dimensions. Researchers in the field of small-group communication have identified the various phases groups pass through in a number of different ways. Gulley and Leathers (1977) present an excellent review of the literature on this subject. We believe that the task and social dimensions, together with the descriptive subcategories of each, adequately describe the primary process factors without overly burdening you as a student being introduced to small-group communication.

There are numerous tasks that must be performed in small-group communication and these occur in a generally orderly process. Figure 1-2 indicates some of the large categories of

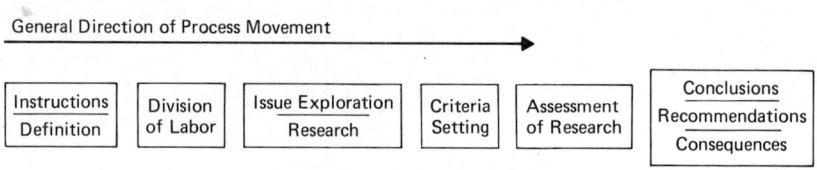

FIGURE 1-2. Task Dimension.

The Nature of Small-Group Communication

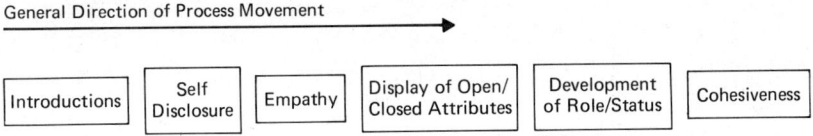

FIGURE 1-3. Social Dimension.

tasks that characterize small-group communication. These tasks must be accomplished through a process in which each segment interrelates with and builds on the other process components. The task dimension is described in detail in Chapters 2 and 3.

The interpersonal interaction that occurs in small-group communication is referred to under the general heading of the social dimension. Numerous interpersonal interaction elements are discussed in this text, but the several large categories in Figure 1-3 are indicative of the elements in the process. The elements of the social dimension work together and build on each other, rather than each element operating as an individual part. For example, a small group will not be a cohesive group until other aspects of the social dimension have occurred and developed the group. Elements of the social dimension are discussed in detail in Chapters 3 and 4.

It may be helpful for you to view together the three charts showing the process aspect of communication in general, the task dimension, and the social dimension (see Fig. 1-4). The task and social dimensions of small-group communication tend to parallel the process flow of the general communication model.

Purposes for Small-Group Communication

Many factors may influence the occurrence of small-group communication. In this text we will refer to them as the *purpose* for small-group communication. Other writers have referred to such factors by other titles and with many different divisions. For example, these could be called functions rather than purpose and the functions could be broken down as persuasion, therapy, social relations, conflict resolution, and decision making/problem solving (Burgoon, Heston, McCroskey, 1974).

Fundamentals of Effective Group Communication

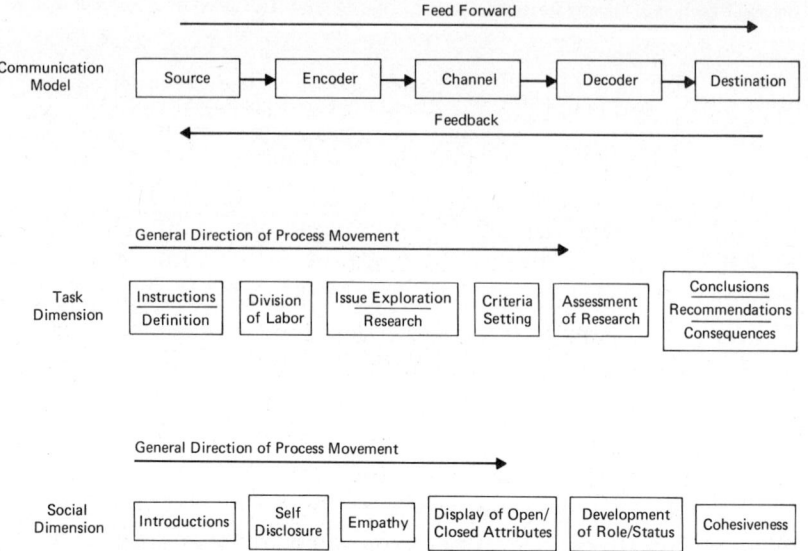

FIGURE 1-4. Process in Small Group Communication.

As mentioned before, this text considers three broad categories of purpose: fact finding, information sharing, and decision making. The compelling motivation for the occurrence of small-group communication may or may not be known. We have described also how at times hidden reasons operate to trigger small-group communication. For our discussion, we will focus on these three broadly stated categories of purpose. The three general purposes we deal with in this text are closely related and even interrelated, but they are separated below to facilitate explanation.

Fact Finding

Fact-finding small-group communication occurs when a small group of individuals forms for the purpose of discovering or clarifying factual information. Groups formed for this purpose usually report back to a larger or parent group that has created the fact-finding body. The larger or parent group is usually the decision-making body and thus the fact-finding group does not have decision making as its primary purpose, although the re-

The Nature of Small-Group Communication

sults of the findings of the group will undoubtedly affect the decision-making body. Fact-finding small groups are often referred to by several different descriptions, including fact-finding team, investigative committee, research team, and the like.

The fact-finding group is by nature very much task oriented. It has a very specific purpose, usually fairly narrowly defined, and often a tight time schedule. In such a setting, the members of such a group will frequently divide specific task responsibilities and do much of the work independently. The group meets occasionally to give individual group members a chance to compare notes and make certain that the group purpose is being met.

A good example of the fact-finding type of small-group discussion is the investigative team concept used by the National Air Safety Board in the case of an airplane crash. Whenever an airplane is involved in an accident, this government agency is responsible for sending an investigator to determine the facts in the case. When there is a crash or accident of a large commercial airliner, the agency usually forms an investigative team to accomplish the fact-finding mission. These officers will work individually and cooperatively to prepare a fact-filled team report to the parent agency, which has the decision-making responsibility.

Legislative bodies such as the U.S. Congress also use this type of group with some frequency. The Watergate Committee, Assassination Investigation Committee, Ethics Investigating Committee, and many others have received wide public attention through the media. These groups have served as fact finders for the larger house of Congress, either the Senate or the House of Representatives. The fact-finding group researches the issue or circumstance and then reports as a group to the full body for action, if necessary.

Information Sharing

Information-sharing small-group communication occurs when small groups of individuals meet on a formal or informal basis to share information on a topic with a specific purpose. The group is simply interested in sharing the ideas, information, or perceptions of various members. A variety of formalized settings use information-sharing small-group communication:

Staff Meeting

This arrangement brings together *a group of staff members in an organization, or a similar group with common interests to share or disseminate information.* This arrangement is frequently used by managers in organizations to provide a communication link with subordinates. The staff meeting permits the manager to disseminate information to subordinates and it also provides an opportunity for the subordinate employees to share information with fellow employees and with the manager. This technique also provides for communication exchange relative to the disseminated information so that it helps to sharpen or clarify potentially misunderstood information. When the manager shares information with subordinates and receives the subordinates' reactions, this is considered feedback and a positive aspect of the information sharing that occurs in a staff meeting.

Study Group

This is used to provide *a small group of individuals with an opportunity to come together to study issues.* Many different types of study groups have sprung up in recent years. For example, a group concerned about some type of environmental pollution might form a study group to delve into detail on a particular environmental issue. Hobby groups interested in certain arts and crafts may form study groups to permit participants to explore in greater detail the particular skills involved in an art or craft. These groups usually have a limited information-sharing purpose and occasionally are very short-lived.

Briefing Sessions

The briefing session is *an opportunity for an individual or group of individuals to present information to a larger group.*

The Nature of Small-Group Communication

Certain government organizations, such as the military, frequently use a briefing-session format. This is also used occasionally by business, industry, education, or other types of organization. Press conferences may also be handled in a manner similar to the briefing session.

The purposes behind such activities are usually to share specific information with a specific audience group and to provide the audience group with an opportunity to obtain additional information through questioning. For example, if a new industry were moving into the local community, an industry representative might attend a meeting sponsored by the local chamber of commerce. At this meeting, which would be in the form of a briefing session or press conference, the industry representative would present the basic information concerning the building plans of the industry. Members of the local community, press, or others who would be in attendance at the briefing session would be given the opportunity to question beyond that which was provided in the formal presentation. The chamber of commerce president might make several remarks concerning the value of the new industry to the local community. The mayor of the community or a local political figure would also probably be given an opportunity to make comments relative to the role of the local government in working with the new corporation. Thus, two or more individuals are involved in information-sharing discussion with a large group.

Decision Making

Decision-making small-group communication occurs when a small group with authority for making decisions meets with the purpose to form a specific decision. As was stated earlier, the various purposes of fact finding, information sharing, and decision making are all interrelated. Frequently, decision-making groups only operate after fact-finding or information-sharing groups have functioned to provide adequate data on which decisions can be built. There are numerous types of decision-making groups, some of which are identified below.

Committee/Council

A committee/council is *a subgroup of a larger unit and is given specific limited responsibilities in relation to the parent group.* The use of committees or councils is prevalent in all types of organizations in our society. These groups, which serve under the authority of a larger organization, provide an effective means for dividing large groups into smaller working groups. Typically, committees and many councils are of the size that puts them in the category of small-group communication. Committees/councils provide an effective way for a large group to subdivide into smaller manageable working units that will more efficiently carry out the work of the parent organization.

Committees/councils usually are assigned very specific and limited responsibilities. Often they are charged with the investigation of a problem and the development of plans or recommendations for consideration of the larger body. The committees/councils then function in a preliminary decision-making capacity as they review particular problems and attempt to arrive at the best possible solutions. Their recommendations, in the form of a committee/council report, are then submitted to the larger deliberative body for final decision making.

Committees/councils, as subunits of larger organizations, are occasionally assigned larger and more permanent areas of responsibility. Sometimes a large organization will transfer the final decision-making authority for certain types of problems to a committee/council, which in this case functions as a standing body to deal with all related issues that come to the parent organization, as well as any special tasks that the larger organization might specifically ask of the committee/council.

Task Force

Occasionally organizations use a specific subgroup, *one responsible for the performance of a specific task that normally does not involve continuing responsibility.* The task force differs from the committee/council in that it is temporary and its responsibility is highly specialized. A task force may also be more action oriented toward resolving a specific problem that confronts an organization and creates the need for a task force that

The Nature of Small-Group Communication

will investigate the problem and work toward short-term or long-range solutions.

For example, let us say an automobile manufacturing corporation encountered a recurring faulty brake on one of its particular car models. The manufacturer might form a task force of engineers representing a variety of specialities to analyze the problem, explore alternative designs for the faulty brake part, and determine the best solution. Once this specific brake problem is solved, the task force would be dissolved.

Colleges and universities frequently use the task force model. Let us say that students and faculty at a particular commuting college are frustrated by the lack of adequate parking. Perhaps a regular campus committee has general responsibility for this as well as other physical facilities. In our example, the students and faculty protest the deplorable parking conditions to such an extent that the administration forms a special student–faculty–administration task force to deal with the urgent problem; the responsibility for parking is thereby temporarily taken from the regular committee and given to the task force. The parking task force provides concentrated intensive study of the situation, analyzes the problem, potential solutions, and chooses one from among them. The task force is disbanded and the regular standing committee resumes responsibility for parking.

Conference

A conference calls upon *a number of elite resources with expertise to come together in one setting to address a problem from various perspectives.* This type of decision-making discussion is often structured for groups that have a fairly large problem that must be addressed from a variety of areas of expertise. Because of this structure, a conference also frequently utilizes the method of multiple meetings rather than one single meeting.

For example, a conference on the problems of aging might have four or five subtitled programs, each a part of the overall conference and with subtitles such as, for example, Special Health Problems of the Aged, Living on a Fixed Income, How to Deal with Inflation, Dealing with Relatives in Your Senior Years.

and Special Legal and Financial Problems of the Aged. In this hypothetical conference the five subgroups would meet to explore the particular problems defined and then gather together for several plenary sessions, meetings designed to bring all of the divergent groups back together for a joint meeting, to deal with the topic in its overall context.

The term "conference" is also used in a very small-group context in a manner similar to an interview with its purpose the discussion of a very specific matter. For example, an employer may wish to have a conference with a subordinate employee to discuss certain phases of the employee's work. Or, an executive might know two or three individuals in the organization who have unusually good concepts of a particular problem area of the organization. The executive would ask to have a conference set up with these individuals to provide an opportunity for small-group exchange on the problem area. The executive is then better equipped to make a decision that will solve the problem.

In any kind of conference, small-group communication plays a prominent part. In the larger conference setting, individual speakers may make formal presentations, but a substantial amount of the conference activity toward problem solving will be generated by the participation of individuals attending the conference. Normally the participation is designed to occur in the small-group discussion setting. In the case of the second definition, the conference will occur in a close, almost one-on-one small-group setting with significant interaction among those participating.

Boards

A board is typically *a group of elected or appointed officials who function collectively as the legal authority for an organization responsible for establishing all policy for the organization.* A variety of kinds of boards function as decision-making or policy-making bodies for organizations. Colleges and universities typically have a board of trustees, a board of regents, a board of overseers, or some other such board that is the policy-making body for the institution.

Policy-making bodies are normally relatively small groups of

The Nature of Small-Group Communication

individuals who meet in a deliberative assembly format to discuss the problems and potentials of the organization in order to establish policies. The policies established by the board are then implemented by the administrative staff of the organization. A board will frequently have committees or task forces at work to deal with specialized problem areas. In these cases, of course, the committees or task forces are subservient to the board that created them.

A variety of special types of small-group discussion are used in special settings. For example, in education a case study method of discussion is frequently used. In this setting a group meets and discusses a topic, acting as though the group is a closed/private discussion. In reality, however, a class is observing the discussion for the dual purpose of critiquing the discussion and learning from observation.

There are also many group arrangements that are used for self-improvement or in therapy. These groups have a variety of names, including: training group (T-group), encounter group, awareness group, human relations training group, human potential group, confrontation group, team-building group, and nonverbal awareness group. Although these groups all use elements of the basic principles of group discussion, each has a special set of rules and procedures often highly individualized to a particular group or setting. (These groups have been mentioned here so that you will be aware of their relationship to group discussion, but these special types do not receive elaboration in this text.)

Formats for Small-Group Communication

The format of most small-group communication is characterized as *closed* (private) or *open* (public). In the *closed* format only the participating members of the small group are present. In the *open* format the actual participating members of the small group participate in view of and in hearing of a public gathering of nongroup members who may or may not participate in the small-group communication (see Fig. 1-5). Thus, the

18   **Fundamentals of Effective Group Communication**

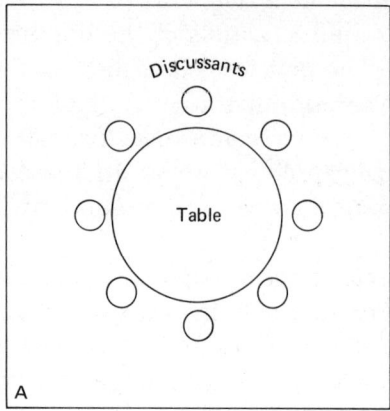

Closed/Private Group Discussion

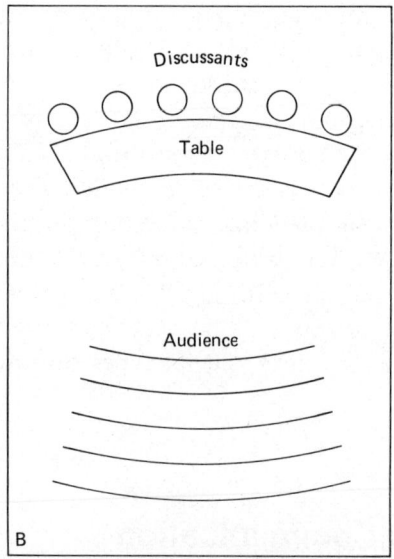

Open/Public Group Discussion

FIGURE 1-5. A. Closed/Private Group Discussion. B. Open/Public Group Discussion.

The Nature of Small-Group Communication

terms "closed" and "open" are also referred to as private or public.

The type of format used in small-group communication frequently depends upon the basic purposes or structure of the group. In recent years increasing legislation of a federal and state nature has made it important for organzations to deliberate in open public settings. There is no firm rule as to when or under what circumstances one or the other format is preferred. Often you will find the small-group communication format dictated by the circumstances of the meeting or by the nature of the group.

Generally, a closed or private group will have several advantages over the open or public group. The most obvious advantages include the following: Individuals feel less restraint in speaking and therefore tend to share more candidly with the other participants; group members are not distracted by the public and have a tendency to give greater concentration to the matters under discussion; and closed groups tend to have more solidarity.

However, because of concern over crucial decisions being made in dark, smoke-filled "back rooms," there is increasing concern to open up meetings to the public. The feeling is that at least where public business is concerned, the advantages of full open disclosure outweigh in importance the natural advantages of a closed group.

In addition to the broad format categories of open or closed small groups, you should be familiar with a number of other terms that characterize the physical setting formats in which small-group communication takes place. Each of the types described in the preceding section of this chapter can occur in one or more of the following formats:

Dialogue

The simplest and smallest unit that can cooperatively communicate orally is a group of two. *When two individuals are engaged in conversation or orally cooperating to share information or to attempt to solve a problem,* a dialogue is in progress.

A dialogue sometimes has a special definition to indicate a format in which two individuals participate in a public dialogue.

In the public dialogue format normally a controversial problem or issue has been established and one speaker makes presentation for and one against the issue. In this public dialogue, following each speaker's formal presentation, the two speakers enter into a small-group discussion on the issue with a public audience. This usually takes the form of a question-and-answer period.

Panel

A panel is a *small group of experts who enter into small-group communication on a topic with a public audience observing the expert discussion.* A panel is one of the most frequent types of public small-group communication. It sometimes provides for each participating expert to make a brief introductory statement before the group enters interactive discussion. When this is done the introductory presentational speeches of the participants are normally kept relatively brief. The panel format should focus on the interactive discussion that will occur among the various expert participants so that the session is not merely a set of individual speeches.

Symposium

A symposium is *a collection of individual presentations brought together in one packaged presentation.* Individual participating speakers make formal presentations before a public audience. The symposium has little direct interaction among the participants, but rather is a format that explores a problem and attempts to achieve a solution through an advance assignment of topics to be covered by individual speeches of the various experts. Each expert in turn presents a formal presentation related to that sector of the problem/solution to which each has been assigned.

Forum

This is *a designation used to indicate that the group will operate in an open/public situation and that there will be opportuni-*

The Nature of Small-Group Communication

ties for the public to interact with the small-group participants. The forum format is used almost exclusively in conjunction with one of the other formats.

In a *dialogue forum* two individuals will engage in a dialogue format of small-group communication for a period of time and then open the dialogue into a question-and-answer session or an open format with the audience participating. In a *panel forum* the panel will operate on the regular panel format for a period of time and then open to public participation through questions and answers with the audience. Likewise, in a *symposium forum* individual speakers will make the presentations in the normal symposium format; following the formal presentations of the symposium, the public audience will be invited to participate in a question-and-answer session.

Hybrid

The discussion formats that we have outlined contain only the basic types that are used. There are numerous methods of developing small-group communication and you will find many of these in practice in a variety of settings. The term "hybrid" is used to apply to *the combination of types and formats that can be used to meet the needs of particular situations.*

When to Use Small-Group Communication

There are many popular sayings that we use in our everyday lives that give some indication of the value of small-group communication. Consider a few of these sayings as they apply to the concept of having small groups discuss issues to attempt to find facts, share information, or solve problems: "Two heads are better than one." "United we stand, divided we fall." "The more the merrier." These quotations can be applied to multiple settings but they all indicate that there is value in groups. The value may be in increased knowledge, or increased resources, or increased merriment; but nevertheless there is value in the group!

There are many occasions when small groups can be very successful and yet there are times when it would not make sense to ask a small group to undertake a task. Smith (1965) devoted an entire chapter to the values and limitations of groups. Cartwright and Zander (1968) review preconceptions about groups, including their strengths and weakness.

We will identify some of the strengths and weaknesses of small groups. Consider these guiding principles in determining when you think small-group communication is appropriate.

Strengths of Groups

Basically groups provide increased resources in terms of manpower to perform tasks and in terms of brain power to generate ideas.

First, consider the increased thought power of a group. Any individual, no matter how bright, has only so much capacity to generate ideas or possesses some fixed amount of knowledge. When you take multiple individuals and put them together into a small group, you multiply and increase the information contained by the group and the potential for generation of ideas is expanded.

For example, Figure 1-6 describes one possible arrangement. A group discussion might include four participants, each with special expertise and knowledge in some particular phase of the whole topic. Four other members of the group may be participants with a good general knowledge and overview perspective of the whole topic. This collection of resources into a group produces considerably expanded brain power, greater than that available from any one individual.

Second, groups provide for additional manpower in making resources available to physically accomplish tasks. For example, groups often find it helpful to subdivide responsibilities to investigate a matter, to determine possible solutions, or to explore ramifications or effects. One or two individuals may undertake those tasks individually but the job will be significantly easier and perhaps better if there are six or eight individuals involved in the task rather than one or two. Thus, if division of tasks is necessary or possible, often a group approach is desirable.

The Nature of Small-Group Communication

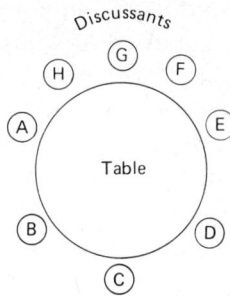

Discussant A — expert on issue #1
Discussant B — expert on issue #2
Discussant C — expert on issue #3
Discussant D — expert on issue #4
Discussant E — person with overview of topic
Discussant F — person with overview of topic
Discussant G — person with overview of topic
Discussant H — person with overview of topic

FIGURE 1-6. Discussion Group: Pooled Brainpower.

For example, Figure 1-7 describes one possible arrangement. Let us suppose that a group of five individuals in a discussion class were assigned to prepare a discussion on a given topic. The group met to map preliminary plans and strategies. Taking advantage of the strength of a group to divide and accomplish specific tasks, the members assigned themselves individual responsibilities. Two members researched specific but separate is-

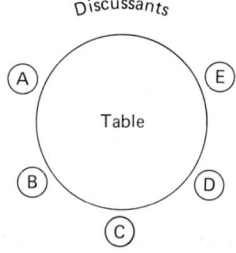

Discussant A — research issue #1
Discussant B — research issue #2
Discussant C — conduct survey #1
Discussant D — conduct survey #2
Discussant E — interview person X

FIGURE 1-7. Discussion Group: Division of Labor.

sues, two participants conducted separate surveys that were needed, and one member obtained an important interview with a valuable resource person. The whole group did not have to perform each of these tasks, yet the whole group benefited from collection of all the data. By dividing the tasks and assigning one task to each, the efficiency of the group was increased greatly.

Third, often the success of information dissemination or of problem solving hinges upon acceptance by those affected. Because of this it is often desirable to involve people in the information dissemination or in the process of finding solutions to problems. This produces a feeling of acceptance on the part of those who are involved in the process. Acceptance is a crucial element to the success of an information dissemination program and it is crucial to the successful implementation of a desirable solution.

For example, Figure 1-8 describes a possible arrangement. Let us suppose that a group of five individuals meet to explore a problem and develop a solution. After carefully reviewing the problem and analyzing many possible solutions, the group cooperatively worked out a solution that had some element contributed by each member. Even though participant A, for example, may not have initially independently supported partici-

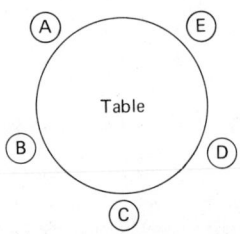

Discussant A — contributes A* to solution
Discussant B — contributes B* to solution
Discussant C — contributes C* to solution
Discussant D — contributes D* to solution
Discussant E — contributes E* to solution

FIGURE 1-8. Discussion Group: Each Member Contributes to the Solution of the Problem.

The Nature of Small-Group Communication

pant B's suggested solution, through the process of give and take in the small group participants A and B and all the others are united in desiring to see the solution work because each has some personal part in the agreed-upon group solution.

Weaknesses of Groups

As with most good things, there are certain disadvantages or problems. This is true of small-group communication. Several of the problems are:

1. A group automatically takes more time to deal with an issue than one individual; thus, the group approach is time-consuming and may sometimes be counterproductive in efficiency.
2. Groups are only as strong as the individuals in the groups. Having a group does not mean that the group will be strong. A popular slogan often used in reference to computers is: "Garbage in—garbage out." It is also true that groups are only as strong as the contributions put into the group by the individuals participating. The old saying, "The chain is only as strong as its weakest link," describes the small-group communication setting.
3. Groups frequently substitute talk for action. There is often a feeling in groups that if you are talking about a problem then you are doing something about it. Mere talk, though it might make members feel good, is usually not enough to get the group job done.
4. Cliques frequently develop within groups that isolate certain individual members. Such an individual can feel lost or unwanted in a group and this is counterproductive.
5. Groups easily get too large. As indicated earlier, approximately eight members are the usual maximum for small-group communication.
6. Sometimes groups are less successful in getting participation in the solution to the problem. This is true because individuals know that there are others in the group and they take the "Let Jane do it" attitude. Some members feel no need to

work toward the solution because they believe others in the group will surely do the work. Thus, the feeling of personal individual responsibility is sometimes lost in a group.

Summary

Small-group communication was defined and explained in terms of its three key component parts. The everyday uses of small-group communication were described. Communication as a process was explained, and the task and social dimensions were discussed as a part of the process in small-group communication.

The three purposes for small-group communication—fact finding, information sharing, and problem solving—were defined and described. Other types of discussion we described were the fact-finding team, investigative team, research team, staff meeting, study group, briefing session, committee/council, task force, conference, and board.

The open (public) and closed (private) formats were defined and described as the two broad categories for formats of discussion. Other formats described were dialogue, panel, symposium, forum, and hybrid.

The strengths and weaknesses of group discussion were enumerated and treated in relation to when to use and when not to use the small-group communication process.

References and Further Reading

BARNLUND, DEAN C., *Interpersonal Communication: Survey and Studies.* New York: Houghton Mifflin, 1968, pp. 3–12.

BORMANN, ERNEST G., *Discussion and Group Methods: Theory and Practice* (2nd Ed.). New York: Harper and Row, 1975, Chs. 1 and 2.

BURGOON, MICHAEL, JUDEE K. HESTON, and JAMES C. MCCROSKEY. *Small Group Communication: A Functional Approach.* New York: Holt, Rinehart and Winston, 1974.

CARTWRIGHT, DORWIN, and ALAN ZANDER. *Group Dynamics: Research and Theory* (3rd Ed.). New York: Harper and Row, 1968, pp. 22–24.

GULLEY, HALBERT S., and DALE G. LEATHERS. *Communication and Group Process* (3rd Ed.). New York: Holt, Rinehart and Winston, 1977, pp. 110–118.
MILLER, GERALD M., *Communication and the Small Group.* Indianapolis: Bobbs Merrill, 1966, Ch. 1.
SHAW, MARVIN E., *Group Dynamics: The Psychology of Small Group Behavior* (2nd Ed.). New York: McGraw-Hill, 1976.
SMITH, WILLIAM S., *Group Problem Solving Through Discussion* (Rev. Ed.). Indianapolis: Bobbs Merrill, 1965, pp. 41–60.
TUBBS, STEWART L., *A Systems Approach to Small Group Interaction.* Reading, Massachusetts: Addison-Wesley, 1978.

Preparation for Group Discussion

OBJECTIVES:
After studying this chapter, you should be better able to:

Appreciate the need for advance planning in preparation for discussion.

Define the planning process necessary in preparing for discussion.

Identify and describe specific planning steps that need to be followed in preparing for discussion.

Phrase discussion questions for optimum clarity.

Prepare physical arrangements for discussion groups.

Locate and evaluate information that may be used in discussion.

Prepare information in an organized system for effective use in a discussion.

FUNDAMENTALS OF GROUP COMMUNICATION[1]

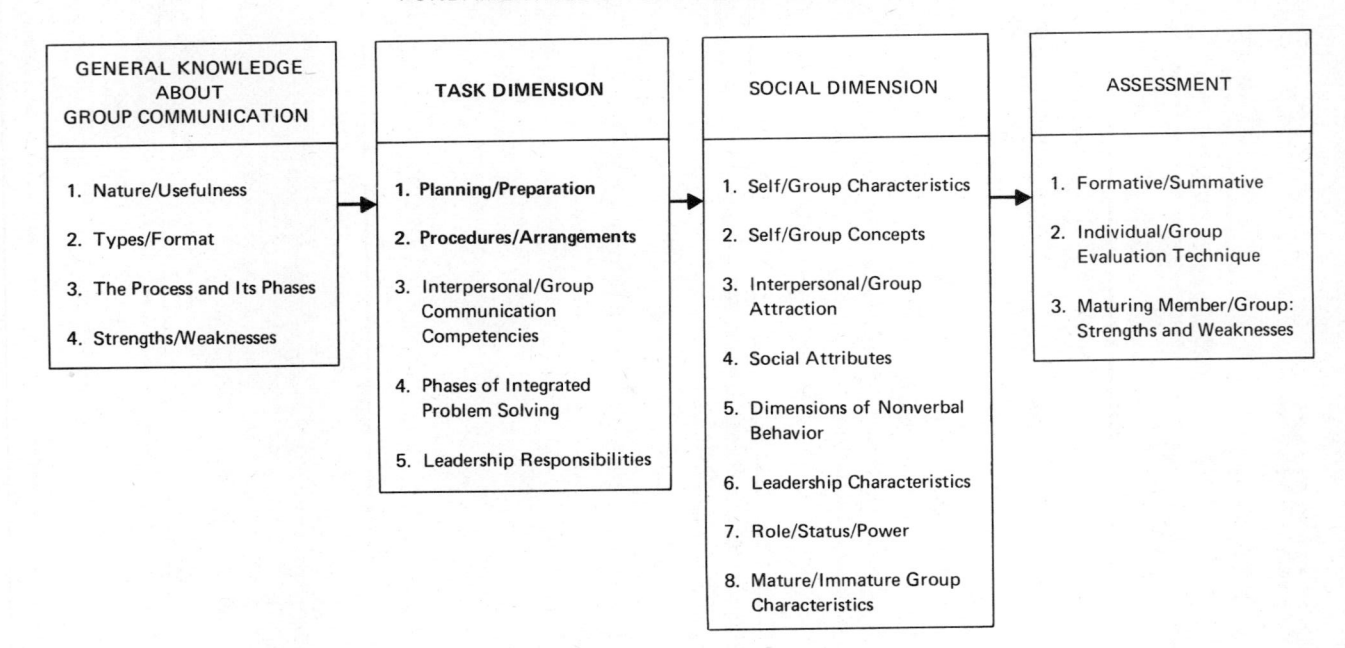

GENERAL KNOWLEDGE ABOUT GROUP COMMUNICATION
1. Nature/Usefulness
2. Types/Format
3. The Process and Its Phases
4. Strengths/Weaknesses

→

TASK DIMENSION
1. **Planning/Preparation**
2. **Procedures/Arrangements**
3. Interpersonal/Group Communication Competencies
4. Phases of Integrated Problem Solving
5. Leadership Responsibilities

→

SOCIAL DIMENSION
1. Self/Group Characteristics
2. Self/Group Concepts
3. Interpersonal/Group Attraction
4. Social Attributes
5. Dimensions of Nonverbal Behavior
6. Leadership Characteristics
7. Role/Status/Power
8. Mature/Immature Group Characteristics

→

ASSESSMENT
1. Formative/Summative
2. Individual/Group Evaluation Technique
3. Maturing Member/Group: Strengths and Weaknesses

[1] Concepts in bold face are emphasized in this chapter.

At this point in your life most of the informal discussions that you have been involved in so far have been conducted with little or no specific advance preparation. In fact, probably most of the formal discussions in which you have participated have also been characterized by minimal advance planning. This chapter will demonstrate for you the importance of planning and advance preparation, and will provide you with an understanding of the essential ingredients of the planning and preparation process.

Although much of the material in this chapter is written to prepare you for participation in discussions in this class, you will find that the planning and preparation process is also applicable to "real world" situations that you will encounter after graduation as you enter your professional career. In the discussion exercises in which you will participate as a member of this class, you will usually be given advance notice and adequate time to go through a detailed planning and preparation process. However, in the experiences you will encounter in your professional occupation you will frequently find that you have little or no notice. Nevertheless, if you are well acquainted with the essential ingredients of the planning and preparation process, you will be able to act quickly to prepare yourself for discussion despite rather spontaneous notice. Although one obviously could not follow the detailed process and procedures in a spontaneous discussion, a person trained in using the planning and preparation process will be able to organize quickly substantially better than the untrained individual.

Preparing to participate in a group discussion can best be viewed as a process. There are two essential ingredients in this process: initial planning and preparation for presentations.

These two parts to the process are explored in detail in this chapter.

The Initial Planning

The elements of the initial planning phase can be labeled as who, what, why, when, and where (see Fig. 2-1). These represent a series of questions that you should raise when confronted with a discussion assignment. Responding to these questions can provide an easy-to-remember organized way for you to complete initial planning for participation in a discussion.

Initial Planning: Who

Discussion is an interpersonal activity and involves human dynamics. Thus, it is crucially important in the very first stage of your initial planning to consider who will be participating in

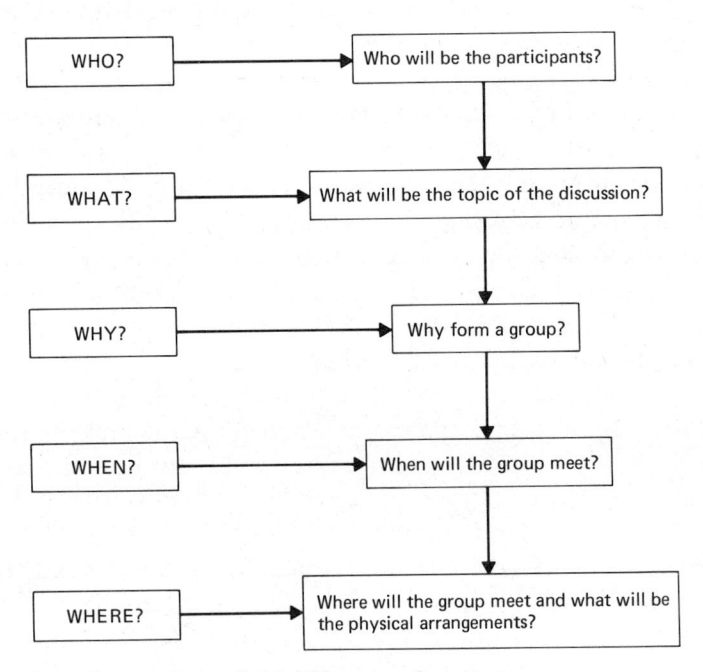

```
WHO?   ──►  Who will be the participants?
                        │
                        ▼
WHAT?  ──►  What will be the topic of the discussion?
                        │
                        ▼
WHY?   ──►  Why form a group?
                        │
                        ▼
WHEN?  ──►  When will the group meet?
                        │
                        ▼
WHERE? ──►  Where will the group meet and what will be
            the physical arrangements?
```

FIGURE 2-1. Initial Planning Questions.

Preparation for Group Discussion

the discussion group. It may be that you will have an opportunity to select the individuals who are to be involved in the discussion group. On the other hand, frequently the participants in the discussion group will be determined by some other person, or predetermined by the organizational structure of a business association or professional group.

For discussions in this class, you may have your groups assigned and you may not have a lot of opportunity to participate in the selection of the individuals who will make up the group. Since this will also characterize many of the group situations you will encounter in your professional career life, even the assigned classroom group is somewhat realistic.

Whether you have an opportunity to select or to participate in the selection of the individuals who will form the discussion group, you still have responsibilities in the initial "who" planning phase. In the group discussion setting, participants can generally be classified as one of two types of individuals, or a combination of the two.

First, let us consider the *task-oriented* individual, *a person whose primary concern is the accomplishment of a task and who shows little concern for the feelings of other participants.* When participating in a group, this type of individual is usually anxious to deal with the issues and zealous in the effort to solve the problem. He or she will be less concerned with the individuals in the group and can often be abrasive in the rush to accomplish the task.

The second type of participant can be generally characterized as *people-oriented, an individual whose primary concern is the relationships among people participating in the group and who demonstrates little concern for the task.* This person is often nondirective and often will allow discussion to drift from the specific topic or task in an effort to build good personal relationships. A complete detailed explanation of these types is provided in Pfeiffer and Jones (1969).

Most individuals participating in a group will have certain characteristics of both of these types, but often you can categorize a participant as being more task oriented or more people oriented. The ideal discussant should be perfectly balanced between task and people orientations.

There are sophisticated survey instruments you can use to assist you in determining whether you are task oriented or people oriented and you could also give the survey instruments to other participants in your group. One such form is the *T-P Leadership Questionnaire* that is found in Pfeiffer and Jones (see page 55, References and Further Reading). However, that procedure may be unworkable in many group situations. Nevertheless, it is possible for you to make general observations of the tendency of people to be task oriented or people oriented. Most of us have a general impression about ourselves and those whom we know well and could broadly categorize ourselves and our intimates.

If you have an opportunity to participate in the selection of the individuals who will be serving as a part of the discussion group, it will be to your advantage to get a good balance between these two types. On some occasions, however, when a discussion group has been formed to deal with a particular problem or accomplish a specific task, it may be to your advantage to attempt to select a greater proportion of individuals who tend to be more task-oriented. On the other hand, if you're in a discussion situation in which you are attempting to resolve controversy or reduce tensions, it may be more advantageous to select participants who are generally more people oriented.

Consideration as to "who" should be involved in a small-group discussion must also be given to the question, "Can this individual make a contribution?" Select individuals who are knowledgeable about and have some interest in the topic, are committed to learning about it, or who have some other valued asset that is needed in the group.

Initial Planning: What

It is important to know the impetus for any discussion group. As an early step in planning you should ask, "What is the purpose for this discussion?" For every group discussion there must be a source of need or a situation stimulating a demand for the discussion. This must be established in the early planning phase since it is at the heart of the entire process.

Having determined the basic source of the need for the discussion, you can establish the purpose generally as fact finding,

Preparation for Group Discussion 35

information sharing, or problem solving—or some combination of these—and you are ready to develop a broadly stated general topic. You should work from a general knowledge of what needs to be discusesd and develop a limited topic that narrows the general area to a specific and manageable subject.

For example, if you determine that the discussion will have as its purpose the sharing of information, then you will need to take the general topic and dissect it into a series of specific small subdivisions. This will enable you to pinpoint subtopics that require the gathering and preparation of information for dissemination to the whole group. Although each participant needs to have a general knowledge of the whole topic, this dissecting process will form a natural organizational scheme by means of which members of the group can take on specific task assignments. This will keep members of the group from duplicating the efforts of others and will provide coverage of all areas. The division of labor by assigning specific tasks to various participants involves using a group efficiently, as described in Chapter 1, Figure 1-1.

In problem-solving as in information-sharing discussion, it is important to take the specific topic and subdivide it so that task assignments can be made to individual members of the group. When dealing with a problem-solving question, gather the information that will be needed to solve the problem, and you will find that often the topic can be dissected into specific tasks of information collection on the various subdivided points. Thus, when the group begins its discussion, a sharing of the information can form the basis for intelligent decision making concerning the best solution to the problem.

If it is determined that discussion will be of the problem-solving type, then the general topic area should be refined to an explicit statement of a specific problem. It will be necessary for you to sharpen, to focus upon, and to pinpoint a specific and manageable problem. This problem, for purposes of a discussion topic, should normally be put into a discussion question.

For example, if the discussion is going to be in the general area of energy resources, this is a broad topic area that will need sharpening and refinement to a specific question that can be handled by a small-group discussion. Unless the topic itself gives focus, the discussion will be too general to be productive. It is useful to phrase the topic for a discussion in the frame of a question, because that will encourage you to pinpoint the topical area and will indicate what you hope to obtain from the discussion as a final result, the answer to the question.

Three basic types of questions are used for discussion. These are discussion questions of fact, value, or policy.

1. A question of fact. The question of fact attempts to establish the truth of something that can be known, and sometimes there is a yes or no answer. For example, using the general theme of energy resources, a question of fact could be: "Which of the new energy forms is most cost effective?" This gives focus to the general theme of energy resources but also it is clear that the discussion will center on cost effectiveness and new forms of energy. This is a question of fact because there are established accepted principles of cost effectiveness, and by investigating the production, distribution, and utilization of new energy forms, it can be determined that one is currently more cost effective than others.

2. A question of value. The question of value attempts to make a judgment about a particular topic relative to a moral, ethical, or other value standard. These questions typically have to do with the rightness or wrongness, the goodness or badness of a particular topic. For example, using the general theme of energy resources, a question of value could be: "Is the use of nuclear energy, given its potential radiation effects, morally defensible?" In discussion on this question, members of the group must deal with judgmental issues involving their attitudes, feelings, and moral or ethical convictions.

3. A question of policy. A question of policy encourages the discussion group to resolve what the group's specific recommendation on an issue will be. This type of question usually includes the use of the word "should" in the phrasing of the question. For example, using the general theme of energy resources, a question of policy could be: "Which of the new energy resources should be funded for development by Congress?" The answer to this question would represent a recommendation for a policy.

The three types of questions outlined above tend to operate in a hierarchy. A question of fact would not involve elements of value or policy questions, but a question of fact may be considered in dealing with both the question of value and the question of policy. In like manner, a question of value would not include policy question issues, but aspects of both a question of fact and a question of value may be considered when dealing with a question of policy. Thus, a hierarchy exists among these three types of questions.

Some authors, such as Gouran (1974), suggest that the basic question types should include questions of conjecture; that is, a question that projects to the future based on a hypothetical position. Tubbs (1978) includes questions of definition. There are other ways to form discussion questions, but the general categories of types identified here should help you focus your discussion topic.

Initial Planning: Why

Participants need both an initial plan of what will be covered in a discussion, and an awareness of what precipitated the discussion. Knowledge of the background and the reasons that created the need for the discussion will help them to have a better understanding of the entire discussion process. In the class situation the "why" aspect is often answered by the need for practice in discussion techniques. Thus, this may not be an important consideration for in-class discussions. In discussion settings outside of the classroom, however, the "why" of a discussion is an important consideration that provides perspective for a discussion participant.

You may have heard the term "hidden agenda." This term is used to identify the situation in which a person really wants to accomplish discussion of a very specific issue in a meeting, although that specific point will never appear on the agenda for the meeting. Yet, during the course of the meeting, the individual will make certain that the issue is discussed and, hopefully, obtain the desired result. The issue was not on the formal written agenda but was hidden; thus, the term "hidden agenda." This can occur in group discussion assignments, too, and your being sensitive to the "why" of a discussion can help alert you to hidden agendas.

Groups usually have a "reason for being" and individuals are usually members of a group for some particular reason. A more detailed discussion of why groups form is provided in Chapter 3, Psychological Aspects of Group Communication.

Initial Planning: When

Some attention needs to be given to simply agreeing to a meeting time for discussions as a part of this class. The group will probably have a time assigned to present the group discussion in class. However, it may also be important for members of the group to get together outside of class and it will be important for you to arrange meeting times, and to make certain that the schedule suits as many of the participants as possible.

As you plan toward presenting a discussion in class, you may want to establish a timetable. This is a good practice for discussions that you will be involved in professionally as well. It is helpful to take the tasks and goals that have been subdivided or established as a part of the planning process and set up a timetable for them. This will assure completion of each task at an appropriate time in the overall planning and development process of a group discussion.

Initial Planning: Where

The group needs to establish the precise location where the discussion will occur. In the class situation you may not have any alternative but your normal classroom. However, in professional situations you may have the opportunity to select meeting locations.

One of the specific things you should keep in mind in choosing a location is to use an agreeable one. For example, if you lived in a metropolitan area and you were setting up a group discussion for a local civic organization, you would want to pick a location that would be central for all individuals. In a different situation, if you were in a business and were arranging a group discussion of various staff members, it would be important for you to consider the physical location in the facilities where the actual discussion meeting was to occur. Sometimes, setting a meeting in a conference room adjacent to an executive's office, for example, may serve to either intimidate or enhance the participation of group members. Geographic location is important when planning the location of a group discussion meeting.

Insofar as possible, every effort should be made to have excellent facilities available for a group when it is engaged in discussion. The interpersonal communicative interaction that occurs in discussion is enhanced by comfortable surroundings and facilities.

In selecting a room, it is important to consider the size of the group and the size of the room. When possible, small groups should be placed in relatively small rooms. A small group placed in a large room may make members feel lost or lonely and may inhibit a feeling of togetherness and intimacy. On the other hand, providing a small cozy room for a small-group discussion will enhance the feeling of togetherness and intimacy and should provide a more productive discussion.

Attention should be given to the physical setup of the room and the placement of individual members. One consideration is whether or not to use tables and chairs or chairs only. In your class situation, you may have to use armchairs because that will be all that is available. In most "real life" settings, however, a small-group discussion will be improved if individual members are seated in chairs placed around a table. The various arrangements for setting up chairs and tables are:

Face-off

This type of seating arrangement puts members face to face with each other and encourages close interaction (see Fig. 2-2). However, the structure does not pull the group together but rather tends to put members in confrontation with the individual directly across the table. This type of seating arrangement is used frequently in negotiation settings.

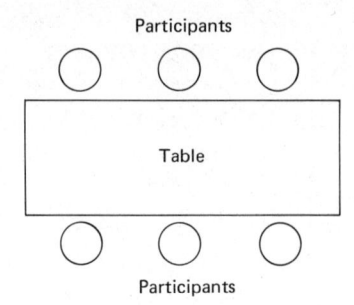

FIGURE 2-2. The Face-Off.

Head Man

This organizational arrangement is similar to the face-off seating arrangement, with the addition of an individual at the head of the table (see Fig. 2-3). This seating plan tends to automatically focus the discussion toward one person. It is often used when one individual desires to have an authoritarian relationship in the small-group discussion.

"Look at Us"

This seating arrangement is best used in a public discussion situation in which discussion participants are basically speaking to an audience rather than to other members of the discussion group (see Fig. 2-4). In this arrangement, each individual discussion participant faces the audience. It does not provide an opportunity for the discussion participants to face each other or to even look easily at each other. This type of seating arrange-

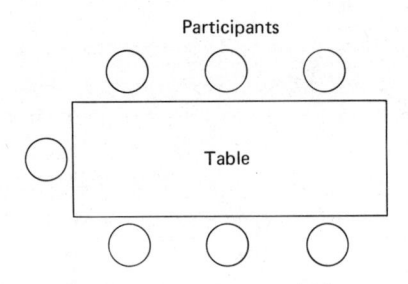

FIGURE 2-3. The Head Man.

Participants

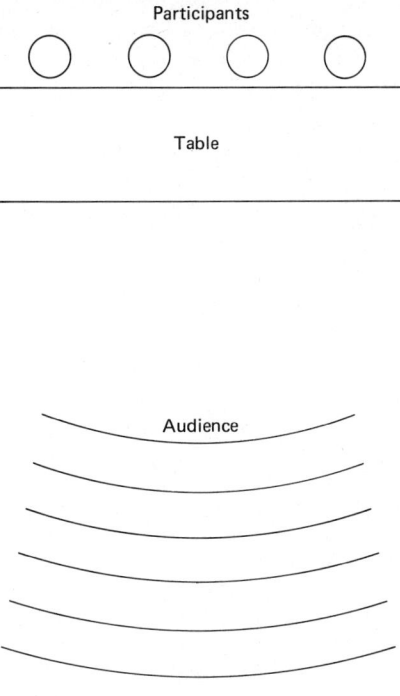

```
  ○   ○   ○   ○
┌─────────────────┐
│      Table      │
└─────────────────┘
```

Audience

FIGURE 2-4. The "Look at Us."

ment should only be used in public discussion settings in which an audience is present.

"We're All in It Together"

This seating arrangement represents the most desirable plan when a group is working in a closed setting and on an equal basis (see Fig. 2-5). These arrangements provide for good visual contact among the members of the discussion group and place each member in such a position that he or she feels equal with all other participants. These arrangements do not put the focus on any particular member of the group.

Physical arrangement recommendations are based on observation of experience with what works well and on the results of small-group research. Hare and Bales (1963) have reported the results of research on physical seating arrangements and inter-

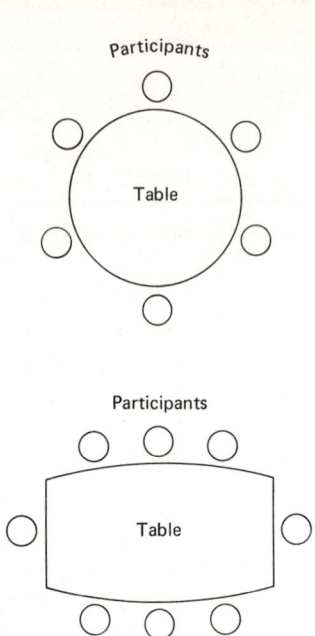

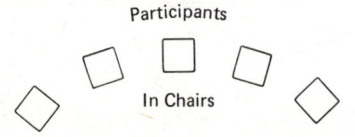

42 **Fundamentals of Effective Group Communication**

FIGURE 2-5. We're All In It Together.

action in the group. Shaw (1971) discusses the results of research on physical arrangements in small groups. In general, the research demonstrates that a strong relationship exists between physical setting/seating arrangement and various aspects of communicative interaction (Gulley, 1968).

There are a few other general factors that you should consider when planning the location of your discussion group. There should be as little noise as possible. Distractions might include exterior hall noise, the possibility of a loudspeaker coming on unexpectedly in the room where the discussion is occurring, and pedestrian traffic that might pass through the room during the discussion. Every effort should be made to eliminate these distractions; if that is not possible, group participants should be made aware of these possible interruptions prior to the discussion in the hope that their preparedness will minimize the effect.

Other factors to consider in setting up the physical location of the group discussion include the availability of good lighting, comfortable seating, and pleasant decor and surroundings. In the "real world" professional setting, it is usually desirable to have ice water and cups available and a pad and pencil placed before each of the participating members for their convenience during the discussion.

Preparation for Presentation

A group should begin by taking its assigned general topic and by dissecting that into subheadings of manageable units. This should be done by the entire group, if possible, but it is sometimes assigned to a designated leader. Each individual member also should consider possible subcategories of the main topic or theme. Once subcategories of the main topic have been identified, the group should assign specific responsibilities for covering the various subpoints, thus distributing the work load and making certain that all aspects of the topic will be covered.

Gathering Information

Taking the topic as a whole and any subparts to the topic that may have been individually assigned, each individual discussion participant should begin organizing individual thoughts by reviewing existing knowledge. Each person will likely have some knowledge growing out of past experience on most any subject. This basic background knowledge can be used as a beginning point. It is helpful to take time to put some existing knowledge on the general topic in writing in brief notes so that you will have some guide to determining the specific points that will need research.

After completing a brief outline of your existing knowledge by subpoints, you should begin your search for new information. A variety of sources will yield information and these are usually categorized from the general to the more specific. These categories of sources of information are:

Encyclopedia-type Works

The most general type of information is usually contained in encyclopedia-type books. An encyclopedia itself deals with topics in a very general way by broad topical categories but it often has dated information. However, it can be very helpful in supplying broad background information on a particular topic.

There are specialized encyclopedia-type books, too. Some of these encyclopedic works provide very detailed information and are often used as reference works to obtain very specific data. For example, an almanac can be a valuable source for specific data on topics such as population, geography, elections, economics, politics, sports, religion, education, and others. A variety of "Who's Who"-type indices give biographical information of a specific type. Also such books as the *Guiness Book of World Records*, another encyclopedia-type book, offer specific statistical information to use as reference.

Books

General books that are available in libraries can be located through use of the card cataloging system. Books, however, provide general information and often contain dated information. A book is usually written about one year before it is published and distributed, and is therefore not a good source from which to obtain recent statistical information. You will find that books are most useful as general background reading to assist you with thorough understanding of broad topics.

Magazines

Weekly news magazines such as *Time*, *U.S. News and World Report*, and *Newsweek* are valuable sources of information on current issues. Because these magazines are published on a weekly basis, the information contained in these articles is al-

Preparation for Group Discussion

ways current. Magazine articles are indexed in the *Reader's Guide to Periodical Literature,* which you will find in your library's reference or periodical section.

A large number of professional journals are published by professional organizations on a monthly, quarterly, or other regular basis. These journals contain detailed and sometimes complicated articles that are often difficult reading for laymen who are not trained in a particular academic field. However, you can sometimes obtain valuable information through consulting these publications. Although these journals are indexed in a variety of publications, one of the most important index publications is *The Education Index,* which you will find in your library's reference or periodical section. (If you need assistance in locating specific information in your library, the reference librarian or other library assistants are usually available in most libraries to assist the library patron.)

Pamphlets

Many local organizations and agencies offer a large number of educational pamphlets that they will make available to interested parties. If the topic of your group discussion entails consideration of energy resources, for example, you may find a large number of local agencies that would have some pamphlet information. For example, a local environmental protection society might have published some pamphlets concerning energy resources and environmental concerns. A local society of the National Audubon Society might have pamphlet information available dealing with the impact of energy resources on wildlife. Local entrepreneur businessmen who might be marketing new forms of energy utilization such as solar heating or wind energy may distribute pamphlets praising the particular energy form.

Many college and university libraries attempt to maintain collections of government pamphlets and documents from government agencies. These are normally kept in libraries in what is known as a vertical file, and libraries often have indices to the aids that are available in such vertical files. Again, if you need help in locating this type of information, don't hesitate to request assistance from a library staff worker.

Personal Contacts

In most communities there is a large reservoir of information to be gleamed from professionals with expertise in topics selected by students for group discussion in class. Obtaining information from personal contacts can be difficult because of the short amount of time that is often available and the difficulty of reaching busy professionals. However, you should not overlook this as a possible resource, and if you can make contact with professionals in your local area who could be of assistance in providing information to you, you should make every effort to do so. A telephone call will often succeed although you may have better luck with correspondence if you have sufficient time to write and wait for a response.

Recording the Information

In your search for information from the various sources that have been described in this chapter, you will need to establish a plan for recording and organizing this information. Students generally record information as they obtain it in continuous form on regular notebook paper. This will often result in a large number of notes related to different subtopic areas, all contained on several loose-leaf sheets of paper.

A preferred way to keep notes is to organize the group's subheadings or subtopics. As you record information from the various sources, record this information on 4 × 6 note cards. These note cards should contain the type of indexing information that is included in Figure 2-6. If you will record your information in this way you will be able to organize your note cards by the various subheadings areas, and the information will be much easier for you to use in the actual discussion.

There are several guidelines that you should follow when recording information in preparation for a group discussion.

1. Be concise. The fewer words you record, the easier it will be for you to capture the essence of the quote. If you record

Preparation for Group Discussion

```
                                    SUBHEADING

    Source: "Article Title," Magazine Name, Date, page number(s).

            "Quote verbatim . . ."
```

FIGURE 2-6.

a lot of information on one card and fail to digest it into a very concise statement, you will find that although the card contains a lot of information it will not be useful to you in the actual discussion. Discussions flow quickly and you must be able to reference your material quickly and quickly insert your information.

2. *Be clear.* You should leave plenty of white space on the card so that the essential content or point to be made from the card can be quickly recognized and obtained for use in the discussion. In the quick flow of a discussion with individual participants actively engaged in making their contributions, you will not have time to search through a card with a long comment, and you will not have time to decipher illegible handwriting or a marked-up note card that cannot be quickly and easily understood.

3. *When in doubt, record the information.* As you are searching through the resource material for information to use in your discussion, it is a good principle to record more information than you think you will need. If you think a particular item might possibly be useful, it is better to record it at that time rather than to wish later that you had done so. At midnight the night before your assigned discussion in class the next day, it would be unfortunate for you to be wishing you had the information that you remembered reading in an article but that you failed to record on a note card. So, record information if you think it might be used. It is better to have too much than too little.

Evaluating the Information

The discovery and recording of relevant information is of little value unless that information is carefully screened and evaluated. Many people believe that if something is stated in print—in a book or a magazine—then it must certainly be true. Unfortunately, that is not the case. While most printed information is generally accurate and not specifically intended to deceive the reader, there is definitely a need for the discussion participant researcher to carefully screen information intended for use.

For purposes of discussion in this text, let us divide basic information into two types: basic statements of fact or opinion, and statistical information. In the following paragraphs you are given some guidelines for assessing the strength and integrity of your information.

General Criteria

It is difficult to assess in meticulous detail every piece of information you collect for use in a discussion. To dissect every piece of information and apply every criteria to each piece of information would be carrying to an extreme a concern for good unquestionable information. Not every criterion can be relevant to every piece of information. An awareness of these general criteria and their consistent application as appropriate to each piece of information you desire to use will maintain good quality control over your information.

1. Source credibility. Individual people, organizations, magazines, newspapers, or other information sources frequently have an existing level of believability. This credibility is a reputation, and it can be high or low, good or bad. In dealing with newspapers, for example, the *New York Times, Christian Science Monitor,* or *Louisville Courier-Journal* all enjoy excellent reputations as highly believable newspapers. Each has a long tradition of excellence that permits you to quote material, confident that most people will tend to accept information from sources such as these. What is true of newspapers is also true of

Preparation for Group Discussion 49

other types of sources. Magazines such as *Time, Newsweek,* and *U.S. News and World Report* are a few examples of trustworthy, credible magazines.

Prominent public individuals develop public reputations as more or less believable people. Organizations also sometimes have high credibility as sources of information. For example, in obtaining specific information in disaster or war situations, the American Red Cross has consistently demonstrated itself to be accurate and believable.

Source credibility is only a general indicator of information acceptability. For example, highly reliable sources may sometimes report available information accurately, but that information itself may later prove to be incomplete or incorrect. Nevertheless, using sources with excellent reputations is your best procedure and should make you reasonably confident about your information.

2. *Information recency.* As a general rule, people like to have the latest word on any subject. Our society has become accustomed to up-to-the-minute information through morning and evening newspapers, and constant radio and television worldwide coverage. Our concern for style in clothing, automobiles, music, and other consumer items is another indication of our interest in recency. Other participants will likely give greater acceptance to your information if it is very current.

3. *Information consistency.* A participant in a discussion has only a limited amount of time available for participation in the group and usually should not become bogged down in a long speech. If you share a small piece of information, the information needs to be acceptable to the other participants basically on face value. If the information is generally consistent with other known information, group members will accept it. If, however, it seems inconsistent with what the participants already know, they will tend to reject the information. In a discussion you rarely have the length of time available that would be necessary to develop an argument to prove a basically unbelievable point.

For example, if you were discussing the need for additional financial support for your college or university, if someone reported that a friend (no particular source credibility) said the school had been offered a million dollars but turned the money away, that information on the surface is unbelievable. It may be true—the money may have been offered with detailed restrictions that were unacceptable to the institution—but it is basically inconsistent with the known need of the school for money. Even if the statement were true, it would take considerable time and explanation to clarify it.

While this type of persuasion is important in other speaking situations, you should generally avoid this in a group discussion and seek to use information that is generally consistent with other known information.

4. Information thoroughness. Although it is difficult to prescribe how much information is enough, you should be aware of the need to be as thorough as possible. The believability of information is tentative and based on a number of factors, so the completeness of information adds to its acceptability.

For example, a quotation from one expert is not as convincing as three citations of generally similar content coming from three different experts. Or, a full organization's backing of a statement may be more valuable than an individual's statement. For example, one medical doctor researcher may have found a certain drug to be effective against a certain disease. The drug is not immediately put on the market for general consumption, but it must be tested in numerous settings by other researchers and the results replicated repeatedly before a full agency of the U.S. government approves the drug for sale and use.

One statistic, or one opinion, or one fact in isolation may be very misleading. You can protect against insufficient information by being as thorough as possible in your own research within the time available.

Statistical Information

Some people are suspicious of statistics because of the saying, "You can prove anything with statistics." One author has written a book entitled *How to Lie with Statistics* (Huff, 1954). Never-

Preparation for Group Discussion

theless, statistics are a very valuable resource for discussion participants.

Statistics represent an attempt to achieve precise information. Statistics quantify in numerical terms and describe in short detail what would take considerable "talk" to reveal otherwise. The *brevity* of statistics is the reason for many of the problems with them, because users of statistics are sometimes not fully aware of the way to interpret them. Bormann (1975) devotes most of an entire chapter in his text to statistics with special concern for helping the student avoid problems in using them.

Statistics are basically of two types: They may *describe* numerically certain general characteristics, or they may sample a general population and make an *inference*. For example, descriptive statistics would include the fact that a college has an enrollment of ten thousand, or that 48 percent of the student body is male and 52 percent is female. These are numerical and percentile representations of a known general population. Descriptive statistics indicate that today's weather was not only "warm" in temperature, but that the high was 70 degrees. Inferential statistics would be used if you sampled some small portion of the ten thousand students and found that one fourth of the sample population preferred pass–fail grading to the letter-grade system. You would infer from the sample to the whole student population and assume 25 percent of the students at your school preferred pass–fail grading. Inferential statistics tell us that there is a 60 percent chance for rain, not just a "good chance" for rain.

Earlier, we mentioned that statistics can be difficult to interpret and apply. Identified below are several key concerns you should be aware of in considering the use of statistics.

1. Accuracy. In assessing the accuracy of descriptive statistics, you should rely on the credibility of the reporting source. In evaluating the accuracy of inferential statistics, however, there are several points of understanding you should have. The inferential statistic represents a generalization from a small sample. Any inferential statistic has a margin of error, called a confidence interval, which describes the odds of the accuracy of the statistic. The margin of error (confidence interval) is usually described as a plus or minus ($\pm$) some specific number. Such a statistic also has a degree of believability (level of confidence) that is statistically determined and expressed in hundredths. Thus, in our example of a sample of your college you found that 25 percent of the students prefer the pass–fail grading system to letter grades, the confidence interval might be $\pm$ 5 with a 0.05 level of confidence. Thus, you would be 95 percent sure that between 20 percent and 30 percent of the students at your school preferred pass–fail to letter grades.

The inferential statistic, properly developed, is still only an inference. It is not exact but only a generalization that is more or less reasonably accurate. It should be used in this way and should not be applied in an overly specific manner.

2. *Sampling problems.* Sampling is an important element in inferential statistics and there are two elements you should particularly note relative to samples: size of sample and possible sample bias. The larger the sample is in relation to the total population, the greater the probable accuracy of the statistic. If you have a population of ten thousand and first sample one hundred and then one thousand, you should have a greater degree of confidence in the results of the sampling of one thousand than the sample of one hundred. There is a point of diminishing return, however, and thus the increased accuracy that would be obtained by sampling five thousand rather than one thousand would probably not justify the expense, time, and labor required to obtain the larger sample. If you know the size of the sample in relation to the total population but don't know the confidence interval, you can make a general judgment about the accuracy of the statistic.

Bias in the sample population can also be a problem. A sample should reflect all aspects of the general population. If, in taking the student sample for pass–fail grading, you sampled only students living in fraternity and sorority houses, your statistical information would be "biased" and would not represent the total student population. Thus, it would be erroneous to use the information from the sample to develop a statistic to apply to the whole student population.

Preparation for Group Discussion

3. Using statistics. Because statistics are specific numerical descriptions of large and complex populations, they run a risk of being used in an oversimplified way. You should use a statistic as one type of support, not as the sole basis for a point. You should be cautious to use the statistic in its special particular sense and avoid misapplication of the statistic to generalizations for which it was not intended.

Another caution is the comparison of statistics. A statistic represents very precise information but it came from a large and complex population. Two statistics standing alone may appear very comparable, but when you analyze where the statistics came from, you may find they really are not comparable.

Because of the power of statistics to consolidate large amounts of information into very compact terms, they have become extremely popular and useful in our society. The use of statistics is especially appropriate in dicussion because of the need for conciseness. All discussion participants should be sensitive to the proper use and the potential for misuse of statistical information.

Final Checks Before Beginning

Here are a few suggestions for you to use as checks before you begin a discussion.

1. Be ready. Group discussions flow very quickly. Many discussions that will be held in your class may be as short as twenty to thirty minutes, rarely longer than forty-five to fifty minutes. With a group of five, six, seven, or eight individuals participating in a discussion, that would mean that each individual participant would have from a minimum of about three minutes to a maximum of about six or seven minutes. The discussion will flow so quickly that you must be totally prepared in order to make your best contributions in such a short time period.

2. Be alert. Mentally you must be on the edge of your seat, ready to participate instantaneously as opportunity presents itself or as the discussion flows into an area in which you have background information or expertise. You may have a particular point that you want to make but if you are not mentally alert, opportunity will pass you by and the detailed planning and preparation you did will have been in vain because you were not alert enough to make your contribution at the appropriate time.

3. *Know your stuff.* You must know your information and material very well. If you have done a lot of research and have all of the information and material before you on nice neat note cards but you do not know the information well enough to make instantaneous contributions, you will not be a successful discussion participant. In the flow of a discussion there is not time for you to fumble through or search through your note cards or papers looking for a comment you remember and that you think you want to use. You need to have this clearly in your mind so that you will know exactly where the information is and so that you can obtain it quickly from your notes to present it to other members of the group for their consideration.

Summary

This chaper emphasized the process aspect of preparation for discussion. Two main phases were described in detail: initial planning and preparation for presentation.

The initial planning phase included a review of the five questions—who, what, why, when, and where—as they apply to the group discussion process. The task-orientation and people-orientation potentials of individual participants were presented. The wording of discussion questions as questions of fact, value, or policy was also treated. Seating arrangement patterns were defined and described under the headings: face-off, head man, "look at us," and "We're all in it together."

The preparing for presentation phase included instructions for obtaining research information on the discussion topic from sources such as encyclopedia works, books, magazines, pamphlets, and personal contacts. Criteria to use in evaluating information were also presented. The chapter included a format for recording information, and a set of rules to follow in preparation for presenting individual contributions during group discussion.

References and Further Reading

BORMANN, ERNEST G., *Discussion and Group Methods: Theory and Practice* (2nd Ed.). New York: Harper and Row, 1975, pp. 97–110.

GOURAN, DENNIS S., *Discussion: The Process of Group Decision-Making.* New York: Harper and Row, 1974, pp. 68–69.

GULLEY, HALBERT E., *Discussion, Conference and Group Process* (2nd Ed.). New York: Holt, Rinehart and Winston, 1968, pp. 69–71.

HARE, A. PAUL, and ROBERT F. BALES. "Seating Position and Small Group Interaction," *Sociometry*, Vol. 26, 1963, pp. 480–486.

HUFF, DARRELL, *How to Lie with Statistics.* New York: Norton, 1954.

PFEIFFER, J. WILLIAM, and JOHN E. JONES. *A Handbook of Structured Experiences for Human Relations Training.* Vol. I. La Jolla, Cal.: University Associates, 1969.

SHAW, MARVIN E., *Group Dynamics: The Psychology of Small Group Behavior.* New York: McGraw-Hill, 1971, pp. 117–136.

TUBBS, STEWART L., *A Systems Approach to Small Group Interaction.* Reading, Massachusetts: Addison-Wesley, 1978, p. 100.

Psychological Aspects of Group Communication

OBJECTIVES:
After reading this chapter, you should be able to:

Identify and describe the psychological aspects of group communication.

Identify and describe the reasons why people join a group.

Identify and describe the five "screens" that compose the psychological screen in group communication theory.

Appreciate the opportunities provided in the small-group classroom experience for testing your "self," and the ways available to you to obtain rewards for being who you are.

FUNDAMENTALS OF GROUP COMMUNICATION[1]

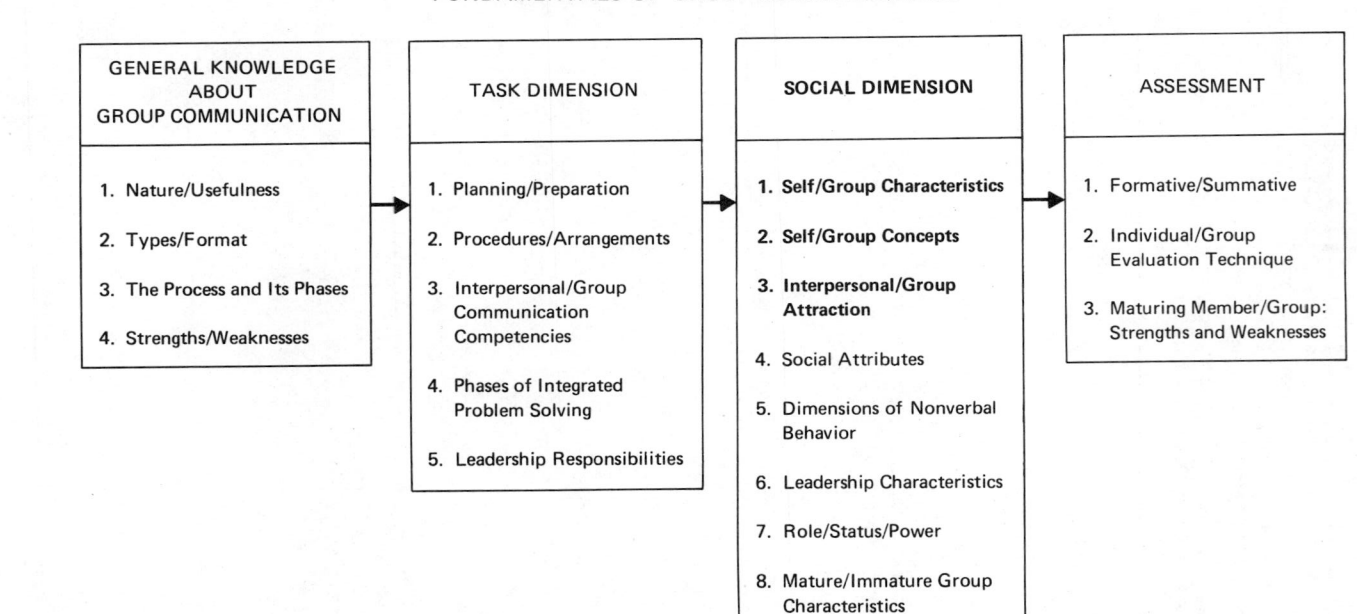

GENERAL KNOWLEDGE ABOUT GROUP COMMUNICATION

1. Nature/Usefulness
2. Types/Format
3. The Process and Its Phases
4. Strengths/Weaknesses

TASK DIMENSION

1. Planning/Preparation
2. Procedures/Arrangements
3. Interpersonal/Group Communication Competencies
4. Phases of Integrated Problem Solving
5. Leadership Responsibilities

SOCIAL DIMENSION

1. **Self/Group Characteristics**
2. **Self/Group Concepts**
3. **Interpersonal/Group Attraction**
4. Social Attributes
5. Dimensions of Nonverbal Behavior
6. Leadership Characteristics
7. Role/Status/Power
8. Mature/Immature Group Characteristics

ASSESSMENT

1. Formative/Summative
2. Individual/Group Evaluation Technique
3. Maturing Member/Group: Strengths and Weaknesses

[1] Concepts in bold face are emphasized in this chapter.

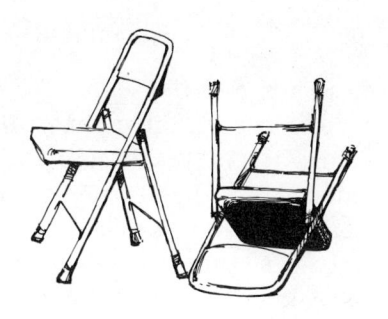

The nation's college campuses during the sixties were alive with protests against the Vietnam War, outmoded social, economic, and political causes, and just about anything that represented the ills of *the* event of the seventies—Watergate. At the same time, the "self-discovery" movement swept across the nation, proclaiming a cornucopia of remedies for our internal ills. Phrases such as self-discovery, self-actualization, self-service, self-enhancement, self-assertion, and self-treatment dotted the literature of college textbooks and the corner newsstand.

Today, the movements toward understanding and engineering the powers of the self are as fresh and vibrant as ever. The heroes of the seventies's search for real selfhood range in temperament from marathoners Bill Rogers, Frank Shorter, Gary Bjorklund, lithe, slight-of-build champions of the road and track, to the heroic figure of "Pumping Iron," the outsized superhuman Arnold Schwarzenegger, and the petite skating star, Jo Jo Starbuck. Each of these people, at the opposite extremes in physical build, perform their individual skills in terms of seaching for and finding inner peace and a state of happiness for their "selves." If the millions of converts to the activities of running, weight-lifting, and winter sports are evidence for the argument for self-discovery, then we are indeed living in a time when strong, self-reliant individualism is a fact of life.

The main theme of today's magnetic evangelists for discovery/awareness/consciousness is learning the "secret of happiness." To use a good Kentucky word, you can "distill" all of the literature, the gimmicks, and the games into one definition: You just need to be who you really are, and who you are is whoever you are when you stop doing all the things you do to be someone other than you are because you are afraid who you really are may not be all right.

Sometimes the search for self-identity can lead to a satisfying experience. At other times, that same search can lead to a holocaust, as in the "Peoples' Temple," Jonestown, Guyana mass suicide. In the broader context of everyday experiences, the journey toward self-discovery and actualization may lead us to organized human behavior and its potential for productivity, "speaking to another human being." Quite often, the dynamics and energy produced by our basic inner drives, wants, needs, and the like emerge through the social organism called a group.

What Makes You Tick?

Eisenson et al. suggest that all motivated behavior operates in a sequence of three steps:

> First, the individual feels a need, stemming from his wants, interests, or purposes. Second, this feeling of need leads him into some form of instrumental or problem-solving behavior. Third, if this behavior is efficient, it achieves a specific end that satisfies the original need. The omnibus term describing this complete sequence is motivated behavior.

The fundamental drives that affect our normal human behavior, and our communication are basic, unlearned drives, present in all of us. Eisenson et al. provides a solid list of human motivations that touch us where we live, especially in our present study of the psychological aspects of group communication:

> 1. *Human beings direct their activities toward the satisfaction of physical wants and general well-being.* They avoid, whenever possible, situations that may bring about physical deprivation, including pain, hunger, thwarting of sex impulses, and a need for sleep. Much contemporary advertising promises these satisfactions, whether from headache remedies, fancy foods, or form-fitting mattresses. An individual can suffer any of these deprivations temporarily, however, and he may knowingly enter into situations which will deprive him for a time if he believes that there will be ultimate satisfaction. The willingness of astronauts to undergo periods of intense training is at least partially explainable in terms of the ultimate respite they know will come at the end of their missions.
> 2. *Human beings normally behave in ways that will lead them*

Psychological Aspects of Group Communication 61

toward success, mastery, and achievement. They try to avoid situations that may thwart, frustrate or disappoint them. Again, however, individuals may often knowingly accept temporary disappointment when there is promise of future success or achievement. Some students, for example, may withdraw from athletic competition if they fear that they cannot "make the team"; but others willingly engage in rigorous drills if they believe that "practice pays off." It is normal to want to "be the best of whatever you are."

3. *Human beings tend to behave in ways that will help them to gain recognition, respect, and approval.* They avoid action that may result in being ignored, looked down upon, or merely tolerated. Even temporary disdain may be accepted by an individual if he feels there is a possibility of gaining lasting respect; tomorrow's cheers will compensate for today's jeers. Those who study social influence on behavior often refer to "status needs," the drives to achieve favorable prominence in one's own social hierarchy. Some groups accord high status to get intellect or creative talent; in others these virtues count for little, but material possessions—costly cars, lavish wardrobes, or unlimited expense accounts—are status symbols. So common is this drive for recognition that "status seeker" is now a widely used label.

4. *Human beings generally act in ways that will lead toward their being loved, and the realization of a feeling of being wanted.* They tend to avoid behavior that keeps them from "belonging," and to indulge in activities that are not intrinsically satisfying—such as going to concerts or attending cocktail parties—if participation will strengthen group ties. Human beings usually prefer the company of others rather than being alone, and prefer to be with familiar persons rather than strange ones. There are notable exceptions, however; explorers may visit isolated areas or strange people, and recluses may shun all human contacts. But such persons may well be motivated in their behavior by other drives which are for them, at least at the moment, more fundamental.

5. *Human beings usually act in ways that will bring about peace of mind, security, and a feeling of release from worry and anxiety.* They try to avoid involvement in situations that create fear, anxiety, or insecurity. Students lacking confidence in their mathematical abilities may avoid science courses; others, feeling deficient in social qualities, may refuse opportunities for group memberships. In some circumstances, of course, individuals may be oppressed by more than one of these concerns, and be forced to accept a lesser, and perhaps temporary, worry in order to put off a more serious one. Thus "robbing Peter to pay Paul" or "choosing the lesser of two evils" are common behavioral guides.

6. *Finally, human beings indicate by their behavior that they*

seek some adventure, new experiences, and zestful living. They tend to avoid boredom and monotony. How much adventure or how many new experiences a person seeks is a highly individual matter. The man who is responsible only to and for himself may often enter into situations that are not only new but dangerous, in his search for zestful living. But the less mobile man, such as the head of a family, tends to suppress his drive for new experiences in favor of mundane security. Generally, however, individuals seek a condition of life with enough novelty to prevent monotony, but not so much novelty that living will be difficult because of the necessity of making continuous adjustments to too rapid change. The appeal of eating in exotic restaurants or of watching adventure programs on television may thus be compensation for otherwise humdrum living.

With these elements in mind, we stated earlier in Chapter 1 that a small group has cooperative interaction through communication with a purpose; this quality makes a "group" of the participants. Shaw argues that a group will vary in the extent to which it rewards its members. Such expectations notwithstanding, the attainment of a goal is the attraction of forming a group. The dynamics of groups vary widely because of the individual behaviors of their members; thus, every aspect of group communication behavior may have its base in such motivational factors as "morale," "admiration," "self-satisfaction," and so on.

In a direct way, we are concerned in this chapter with your discovery of personal and group-centered behaviors that emphasize group learning and group performance. Your interpersonal relationships in your group and the potential group interaction products of effectiveness and attractiveness are our special interest. For it is in the small group that sharp focus is brought to bear on the psychological needs for structure and external direction.

The psychological drives necessary to join and/or form a group are few in number, but significant in scope and impact. First, few, if any, of us can really charge our own "batteries" without meaningful contacts with people we like and trust. The requirements of group interaction and communication activities ask of you an accommodation to and an adjustment with the needs of the others. Quite simply, your main contribution to the morale and cohesiveness of your group is successful, effective interaction. That goal does not come without hurdling or fighting through some serious obstacles. As we suggest in the following, why join a group at all?

Why Join a Group?

Wrightsman cites Schacter (1959) as providing a two-part reply to the question of joining of a group. First, a person may join as a means to an end, his personal ends. Secondly, the group may represent an end in and of itself, fulfilling those items mentioned by Eisenson et al.—"approval," "support," "prestige," and so on.

The central psychological value of group membership may well be that it provides a vehicle for self-evaluation. Festinger indicates that the evaluation of many skills, attitudes, and values can be done only by comparing oneself with other people. That kind of self-evaluation by social and task comparison is a difficult and time-consuming process in the group situation. But, perhaps NOT nearly as deadly a risk as the *avoidance* of contact and purposeful affiliation. There is value in *belonging* as well as great risk.

Psychological Characteristics in Group Discussion

Martin P. Anderson has presented, in Figure 3-1, a broad conceptual model of group discussion, including its essential components, their interrelationships, and the cognitive–perceptual screen involved. While we have concerned ourselves with other processes in Anderson's model in other chapters, we are interested here in the psychological screens that exist *during* the process of discussion and the nature of "screens," as Anderson terms them.

As the model outlines, there are five screens of psychological significance in discussion:

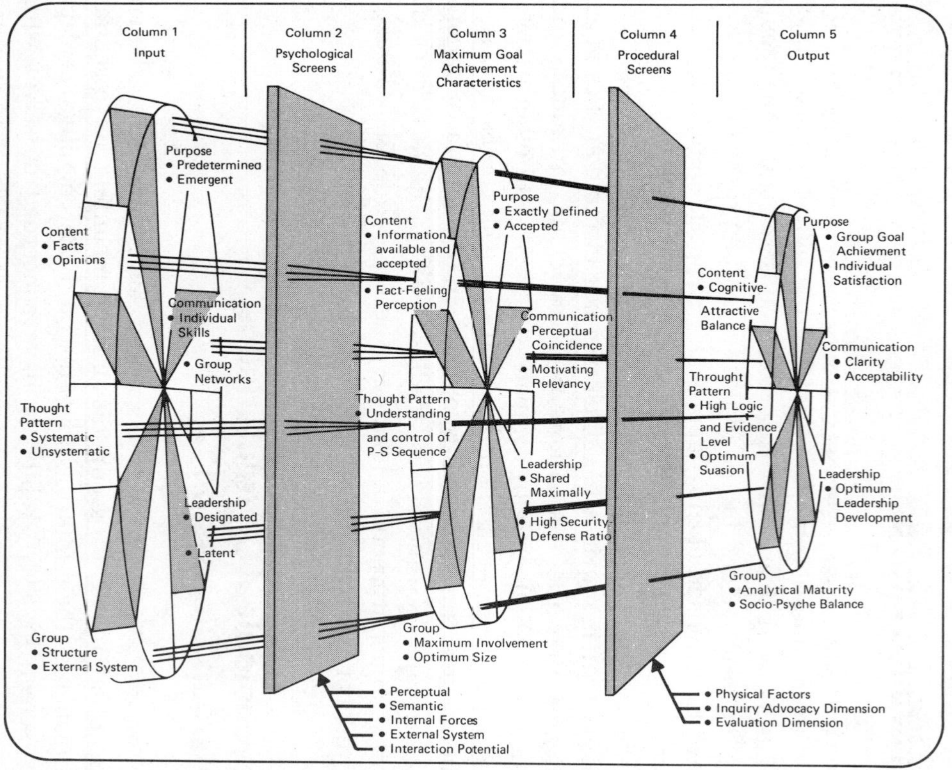

FIGURE 3-1. Model of Group Discussion.

1. Perceptual.
2. Semantic.
3. Internal forces.
4. External system.
5. Interaction potential.

The first screen, then, is one's *perceptual* nature. Your perception is your total realm of experience; that is, the only reality that you really understand. Thus, because everyone else in a small group has different realms of experience (the ways we see the world), it is of paramount importance to deal with the interpersonal and subject differences among people with great care. For example, it becomes extremely important to analyze the members of your group and adapt to their views of the content of the discussion. The ways that we see each other can be both barrier and asset, but the creation of "common grounds" for discussion is essential to healthy interaction.

Our second screen is the *semantic* one. Katz notes that language has functions other than accurate communication. We use language to help or to hurt, to give or to get sympathy, to express our "selves," and for a wide, never-ending variety of other purposes. In interpersonal and group situations, a "liberal" might be defined as a person who holds to extreme views of the far-right or far-left political spectrum. It becomes essential then that we try to communicate and that we do so in similar frames of reference. Language is still an extremely limited system for generating understanding unless the involved parties have a common base of experience.

Controversies abound in our society when groups with different psychological languages and different ways of life attempt to deal with each other. In universities, administrators and faculty seem to always be at odds over class loads, salaries, working conditions, and so on. In business and industry, labor-management disputes are taken for granted as a normal pattern of "getting along." Success in such common communication conflicts requires that we all "walk a mile in the other person's shoes." The difficulties of learning to speak the various languages of our group members are not insurmountable.

In contrast, the difficulty of cross-cultural communication is presented in the humorous stereotyping-commentary of the English writer Nicholson:

> Now when the average German thinks of the average Englishman he . . . visualizes a tall, spare man, immaculately dressed in top hat and frock coat, wearing spats and an eyeglass, and gripping a short but aggressive pipe in an enormous jaw . . . To him, the average Englishman is a clever and unscrupulous hypocrite; a man, who, with superhuman ingenuity and foresight, is able in some miraculous manner to be always on the winning side; a person whose incompetence in business and salesmanship is balanced by an uncanny and unfair mastery of diplomatic wiles; . . .
>
> The French portrait of the Englishman . . . is the picture of an inelegant, stupid, arrogant, and inarticulate person with an extremely red face. The French seem to mind our national complexion more than other nations. They attribute it to the overconsumption of ill-cooked meat. They are apt, for this reason, to regard us as barbarian and gross. Only at one point does the French picture coincide with the German picture. The French share with the Germans a conviction of our hypocrisy . . .
>
> To the average American, the average Englishman seems affected, patronizing, humorless, impolite and funny. To him also the Englishman wears spats and carries an eyeglass; to him also he is slim and neatly dressed; yet the American, unlike the German, is not impressed by these elegancies; he considers them ridiculous; . . .

Although we may have oversimplified the filtering effect of whether word meanings are denotative or connotative in nature, no simple *semantic* formula will solve those cross-cultural communication problems or those that arise in our cultural group settings. Katz argues convincingly that the accurate communication of an objective certainty required by most of us is much more realizable in science than in popular discussion situations. To communicate values, emotions, facts, feelings—these and more are dynamics of the atmosphere of group communication. The best advice is to search for *common ground* in definition of terms, causes, nature of the problem, criteria for solution selection, and so on—all of the basic elements of the discussion process. If there is to be agreement or disagreement, the boundaries should be made clear to all those involved.

Psychological Aspects of Group Communication

The third screen has been described as the *internal forces* of the individual and the group. Every member of your group is striving for some measure of personal satisfaction from the group experience as well as some realization of the goals and purposes of the group. To bring to bear some control and proper use of the group's stability, its cooperative nature, its competitive spirit, and its cohesiveness has significant impact on the behavior of all those involved. Finding one's "middle ground" between the wish to be prominent as an individual and the desire to be a supportive working member of the group will give the group an overall productive nature.

Our fourth psychological screen is the *external system*, the physical, technical, and social environment in which discussion occurs. Whether your discussions take place in the classroom, the church, your dormitory, fraternity, or sorority, or wherever, the very *place* of actual discussion often dictates the *ways* we talk and feel, our inhibitions, and other such influences. The "goldfish bowl" of an in-class discussion, with a peer evaluating group, is enough to stifle a whole group actually prepared to discuss in "private" what they know will be listened to by others. Places, formal and informal, require some getting used to before groups can settle down in the new or varied environment. Realize, then, that your communicative behavior is affected by the location and external circumstances of the *place* where you meet.

The fifth and final psychological screen is the group's *interaction potential*, what Burgoon et al. call homophily (interpersonal similarity) and heterophily (interpersonal dissimilarity). When groups are formed voluntarily, we should expect a high level of effective communication. In the classroom setting where groups are formed arbitrarily (we hasten to note that the same phenomenon exists in business and industry), a length trial-and error period will ensue. A sufficient degree of homophily or a complete lack of it may be the result.

The overriding desire for social interaction among people in groups may well be the number one psychological reason for belonging to them. Burgoon et al. argue for an important principle in that regard:

. . . . the degree to which we are attractive to other people is based not on how often we communicate with them, but what we say to them. Similarly, how attractive we perceive another person to be is not based on how often he talks to us, but on what he says to us. Being sensitive to the orientations when they exist, and being silent about our differences in orientations will generally tend to make us more attractive to other individuals and groups.

In terms of satisfaction with the task-conclusions of a group, the more a person is attracted to the people within the groups and identifies with the group, the more likely he will be satisfied with the product of the group. It is highly doubtful that group members will see to the actualization of a decision unless they had some part in its determination and were satisfied with the decision.

Okay, Where Do We Go from Here?

With the possible exception of the classroom setting, people become involved with a group because there is something in it for them. That something may or may not be tied to the goals of the group. The important, bottom-line concept in understanding the psychological forces working in a small group is that no two members are working for the same reason or to the same degree. Groups grow and mature only as long as needs of the deepest kind are being met.

Closely aligned to the psychological reasons for belonging to a group is the individual's (your) commitment to the group, to the task, and to each other. The span of commitment can range from literally no involvement whatsoever to the "rah-rah" of "let's win one for the group!" Somewhere in between these borders is the individual's own general sense of personal security (self-concept).

One of the most important characteristics of a steady state, psychologically secure person is the tendency to rely on good information as the source of reality. When we have to rely on the *words* of people (in our case, group members) for sound conclusions for our beliefs, then we are probably in trouble.

Psychological Aspects of Group Communication

When we base our beliefs on evidence, new, old, or reinterpreted, then we are not likely to be shaken when personal conclusions prove wrong. The more one works in groups, the more apparent it becomes that not all of one's beliefs, convictions, or attitudes are based on good reasons or relative truth.

It should also be clear that people enter into a group relationship because they need the structure, the intimacy, and the rewards provided by the experience. After the group begins to function, a whole new set of psychological elements come into play, mainly flexibility and adaptability.

The adaptable, flexible member will soon learn to carry out work in the manner desired by the group and required by the configuration of the individuals in the situation. In the classroom setting, the strain toward adaptability and the accompanying threads of flexibility may be stretched to the breaking point for numerous reasons, among them over- and under-achievers looking for "grades," a silent shy member, external restraints from other schoolwork, and the like.

The classroom small group is, in our judgment, one of the most difficult structures of group-discussion types in our society. There are more constraints and hurdles to get over, around, and through than in almost any other circumstance. You will find any number of internal and external obstacles just in getting together outside of class, in working together when no one, teacher or peer evaluating group, is around to force or guide you and your group in working efficiently and effectively. But, here, in the classroom laboratory setting, may well be the best and most concentrated atmosphere for an adjustment with and blending of your motives and drives with the combined psychological interests of an arbitrarily assigned collection of individuals. Practice and supervised, corrected performance should develop learning and communication skill.

Summary

In this book, we are suggesting the fundamental aspects of group communication. In this chapter, we have posited the belief that your personal behavior and the underlying needs, wants, and desires for satisfaction and group success are special and unique contributions. Your primary and continuing involvement in the group will most likely result in an evaluation of both your self-concept and your status in your group.

The small-group phenomena offers you, as noted at the outset of this chapter, an excellent proving ground for discovering your strengths and weaknesses in expressing yourself. The essentials of interaction effectiveness are numerous and significant; the potential for conflict in the group as numerous and as significant. Playwright Eugene O'Neill once remarked that "all life is a struggle, but it is the joy of the struggle that makes us endure."

To realize and act upon the screens of psychological factors in the group situation is to reach for and obtain the maximum in achieving your goals, those of the group, and the potential solutions of the group's tasks. Leavitt argues from the research literature that "independence of action, relative to other members of the group is, in turn, held to be the primary determinant of the definition of who shall take the leadership role, total activity, satisfaction with one's lot, and other specific behaviors." Finally, human beings will resign themselves and cooperate in a group experience if there are clear reasons and obtainable rewards for doing so. This work is the major task of the emerging group.

References and Further Reading

ANDERSON, MARTIN P. "A Model of Group Discussion," *Southern Speech Journal,* 4 (Summer, 1965), pp. 285–288.

BURGOON, MICHAEL, J. K. HESTON, AND JAMES McCROSKEY. *Small Group Communication: A Functional Approach.* New York: Holt, Rinehart and Winston, Inc., 1974, pp. 95–96, 101, 103–104.

EISENSON, JON, J. JEFFREY AUER, and JOHN V. IRVIN. *The Psychology of Communication.* New York: Appleton-Century-Crofts, 1963, p. 224, 245–246.

FESTINGER, LEON. "A Theory of Social Comparison Processes," *Human Relations,* 7 (1954), pp. 117–140.

KATZ, DANIEL. "Psychological Barriers to Communication," *The Annals of the American Academy of Political and Social Science,* 250 (March, 1947), p. 249, 254–255, 258.

LEAVITT, HAROLD J. "Some Effects of Certain Communication Patterns on Group Performance," *Journal of Abnormal and Social Psychology*, 46 (1951), pp. 38–50, as cited in Dean C. Barlund (Ed.), *Interpersonal Communication: Survey and Studies*. Boston: Houghton Mifflin Co., 1968, p. 311.

SHAW, MARVIN as quoted in Bernard Bass, "The Definition of Group," as found in *Leadership Psychology, and Organizational Behavior*. New York: Harper and Row Publishers, 1960, from Robert Catchcart and Larry Samovar, *Small Group Communication: A Reader* (2nd Ed.). Dubuque, Iowa: William C. Brown. 1974, pp. 21–22.

WRIGHTMAN, LAWRENCE S. (Ed.). *Social Psychology in the Seventies*. Belmont, Calif.: Wadsworth Publishing Co., Inc., 1972, p. 400.

The Nature of Interpersonal and Group Communication: A Competency Approach

OBJECTIVES:

After studying this chapter, you should be able to:

Identify and describe interpersonal competencies.

Identify and describe small-group competencies.

Participate and make judgments in actual in-class discussion about techniques for resolving group communication problems.

Use and understand group evaluation forms that emphasize competency in group communication.

Understand and use PIPS—Phases of Integrated Problem Solving.

Appreciate the use of group communication skills that center on effective group behavior through task and process success.

FUNDAMENTALS OF GROUP COMMUNICATION[1]

GENERAL KNOWLEDGE ABOUT GROUP COMMUNICATION

1. Nature/Usefulness
2. Types/Format
3. The Process and Its Phases
4. Strengths/Weaknesses

→

TASK DIMENSION

1. Planning/Preparation
2. Procedures/Arrangements
3. **Interpersonal/Group Communication Competencies**
4. **Phases of Integrated Problem-Solving**
5. Leadership Responsibilities

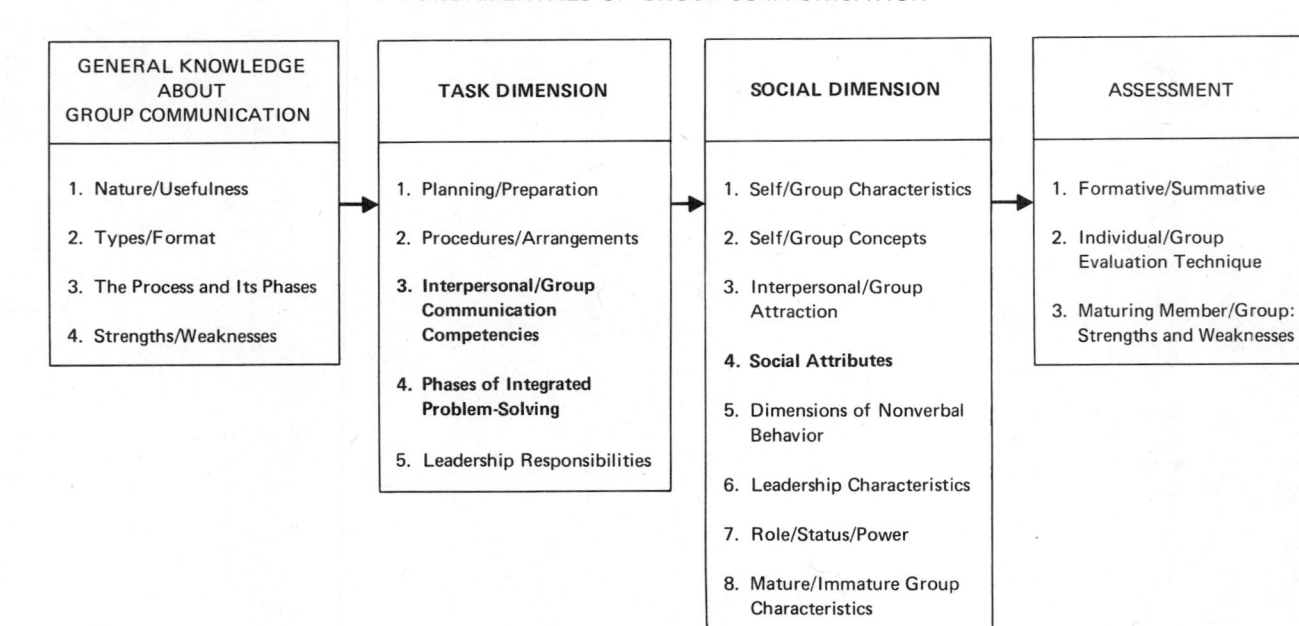

→

SOCIAL DIMENSION

1. Self/Group Characteristics
2. Self/Group Concepts
3. Interpersonal/Group Attraction
4. **Social Attributes**
5. Dimensions of Nonverbal Behavior
6. Leadership Characteristics
7. Role/Status/Power
8. Mature/Immature Group Characteristics

→

ASSESSMENT

1. Formative/Summative
2. Individual/Group Evaluation Technique
3. Maturing Member/Group: Strengths and Weaknesses

[1] Concepts in bold face are emphasized in this chapter.

Futurists have argued that "communication" may replace the "work" concept as the predominant mode of making a living in the near future. Such an argument is not mere fanciful thinking. More and more businesses and industrial concerns are searching for communicatively competent college and trade school graduates to fill available positions in management and public service. Truly, we are living in a society that places a premium on communication skills, regardless of career or job.

For the most part, whatever level of communication skills you may now possess, your skills have been "caught" or "taught" by the "school of hard knocks." Your interpersonal communication skills are the result of everyday learned experiences, some of them effective and some of them not so effective. As you participate and experience the growing pains of how to function effectively in small-group settings, you must invariably learn to function productively on the primary and companion levels of interpersonal communication and small-group communication.

A major theme of our efforts in this chapter is to share with you the fundamental, essential elements of effective small-group discussion. The communication competencies needed for effective interaction in your on-campus and "real world" interpersonal communication experiences are central to your subsequent learning of those small-group competencies needed to function when fact-finding, sharing information, and most significantly, when solving problems.

Interpersonal Communication Competencies

The review of communication literature by Keezer et al. outlines the interpersonal competencies essential for productive living. Let's examine each in turn:

1. *Self-esteem or good self-concept.* Any number of communication scholars and experts in the social sciences have defined self-esteem. Basically, your "self-concept" is a composite of all of the ways in which you see yourself interacting with others and how you weigh the value of those interactions. For example, do you generally like who you are and what makes up who you are? Your intrapersonal image directly affects your behavior with others—your tone of voice, use of clichés, statements portraying the self, and statements made about praise or blame in relating to others.

   To be sure, a strong self-concept affects the ways in which one communicates with others. A weak self-concept distorts one's views of how others see one usually producing feelings of insecurity. The net effects of a weak self-concept are damaging in interpersonal and group communication situations. For example, such a person has difficulty in everyday conversations, admitting wrongs, accepting constructive and destructive criticism, taking issue with others with whom he or she disagrees, and so on. The natural result is a lack of confidence in a broad range of communication settings, including small-group discussion.

   Self-concept is a prime factor in a person's ability to communicate effectively with others. Moreover, self-concept may well be a central factor in demonstrating the necessary group communications competencies to solve problems, share information efficiently, or complete simply assigned tasks.

2. *Self-disclosure.* Self-disclosure is the ability to talk about yourself with others in mutual and adaptive communication situations. To the degree that you can reveal yourself to others in everyday and/or special encounters, you may obtain the

The Nature of Interpersonal and Group Communication 77

result of a mutual feeling of reciprocal self-disclosure from the other person. The conversational and small-group atmospheres can promote either fear or trust in self-disclosure communication. The communicatively competent person seeks to promote trust in "self" with honesty and straightforwardness. Usually, a person without minimal competencies in self-disclosure communication is insensitive to the needs of others, is difficult to approach, is resistant to the suggestions of others, is lacking in objectivity, and is unwilling to understand another's point of view.
3. *Empathy and listening.* Surely, listening must be the most misunderstood competency of them all. How to keep an open mind, to avoid the distractions all around us just to be able to *hear* a message, and how to sort out the real heart of oral–visual message are mammoth undertakings. Like a kaleidoscope in which loose bits of colored glass are reflected by mirrors so that various symmetrical patterns appear, the process of listening is an ever-changing interaction between speaker (1) and speaker (2). The major competency in listening behavior is to be able to decode a message in relatively the same picture of reality as it was sent. The accompanying competency of *empathy* for a speaker is best described as being responsive to the content and the way the speaker feels about what is being said.

The sum total of these interpersonal communication competencies can transfer certain achievements into the small-group communication process. Barrett suggests the concepts of *indentification* as finding contacts for establishing such a base of common communication interests: To communicate interpersonally, it is imperative that you find common bases with the other party, e.g., values, opinions, interests, and so on. Whether there is ultimate agreement or disagreement for what we have thus far listed they are three interpersonal competency areas that begin with the *intra*personal dimension of self-concept and extend to the interpersonal dimension of listening with feeling.

As you progress through these, you will find that you can acquire the power to:

1. Communicate your self and your ideas.
2. Sense an inner feeling of worthiness and success, an awareness of others' needs and feelings, and a general adaptation of yourself to them.
3. Select the best alternative in the personal and social dimensions of interpersonal communication.
4. Trust the other person and care about their feelings during the process of communication.

In interpersonal communication, the competent communicator should be exhibiting the kinds of verbal and nonverbal behaviors that highlight interpersonal "liking," the search for points of similarity, the constant adaptation to the feelings of the other, and the overriding demand to *use* language to communicate the ideas necessary to "get along." Degrees of mutual understanding can result in agreement or disagreement. The success quotient of interpersonal communication rests on the degree of give-and-take between participants in the process. Barrett says it so well:

> You see, all information on the self and interpersonal relations relates directly to communicative competence. As people learn about themselves—and as they accept themselves, they experience growth in the ability to speak with others. The process works back the other way, too. When the aptitude for communicating grows, the total self is positively affected. Speaking is a central and vital part of the self; when the part is strengthened, the whole is strengthened.

Small Group Communication Competencies

The theme of this chapter is to synthesize the important notions of interpersonal communication with small-group communication at the important levels of *competency*. The point is for you to apply the humanistic–interpersonal concepts to the group process. Again, the survey by Keezer et al. of the research provides us with the following list and discussion of *small-group*

The Nature of Interpersonal and Group Communication 79

communication competencies as the second part of the puzzle of communication theory and practice.

1. *Leadership.* Defined in any number of ways and in any number of communication situations, we shall hold to a broad definition of leadership as a "sense of initiative needed in all members of a group to help the group to complete a task." Any kind of verbal and/or nonverbal behavior that helps the whole assemblage of people to reach their group's goal is, in point of fact, leadership. Although some researchers might argue that all group members don't necessarily need to be competent in leadership, it should be assumed that a functioning, continuing group is performing its tasks best when most or all of its members are competent in some aspects of leadership behavior.
2. *Listening.* Defined earlier, listening obviously plays an important role in small-group communication. To be able to withhold judgment, to listen with feeling (empathy), to lend supportive, nonverbal strength to others in a group—these are part of the value of group-centered listening skills.
3. *Assertiveness.* Keezer et al. reviewed the literature and found this *intra*personal quality important for a group member to be capable of stating, interpersonally, personal views and arguing for those views without infringing on the rights of the other group members. It is that interpersonal-group quality of being able to disagree without being disagreeable.
4. *Thought organization.* John Dewey's *How We Think* (1933) argues that thinking in an organized manner in order to arrange materials and statements in a logical sequence is an important skill. Barrett (1968) corroborates the idea in his discussion of public speaking and group-communication skills.
5. *Self-concept.* As in the case of listening, self-concept must be placed in this group-centered category as well. In terms of the assertiveness competency, a self-concept based on strength and confidence should be a continuing source of fresh, new ideas along with the ever-present need to *own* and to take *responsibility* for one's ideas. A weak self-concept in a group

setting leads to guarded, tentative communication and quite often no real communication at all.

To this point, we have identified *eight* distinct communication competencies spanning the interpersonal and small-group communication spectrum. We are convinced that, in order to participate in group-related situations, your awareness of these factors is essential to giving and getting the most from a group experience.

The speech communication profession, individually and as an organizational structure, has yet to comprehensively deal with the establishment of communication competency testing and measurement. The day is not far off when we may be able to administer a battery of varied tests and evaluation forms to audit, as accurately as humanly possible, a person's group skill level with subsequent recommendations for improvements in group communication behavior.

Our immediate concern is to suggest the ways and means that you can go about the task of translating skills in interpersonal communication to the more specialized skills required for group communication. Using the interpersonal competencies as a base, we will suggest a group-centered core of competencies:

1. *The need to learn the differences between individual versus group judgment.* Shaw's review of the research shows that, in general, group judgments are seldom less accurate than the average individual judgment and are often superior. The kind of group task may determine whether a group judgment will be superior to individual judgments. But, in the main, a group judgment does exceed the average individual performance of group members, but does not necessarily exceed that of the most proficient member of the group.
2. *The need to learn the differences between individual versus group problem-solving.* Again, Shaw's review of the research indicates that whether groups or individuals are more effective depends upon past experiences in problem solving, the kind of task involved, the process under investigation, and the measure of effectiveness. In summary, groups are more effective than individuals in tasks that require a variety of

information, which can be solved by adding individual contributions, and which require a number of steps that must be correctly completed in a definite order; individuals are better in tasks that call for centralized organization of parts. Groups perform better than individuals when the process is learning or problem solving, but not necessarily when the process investigated is judgment. These conclusions are based upon measures of outcome; when the measure of effectiveness is the amount of investment per man, individuals are generally shown to be more efficient.
3. *The need to be aware of the "risky shift phenomenon" in group decision making.* Ziller (1957) found that decisions made by group-centered decision-making groups were more "risky" than decisions made by leader-centered groups. The effect is partially explained by a sense of decreased personal responsibility for a decision in a small group (hence a greater willingness to make a risky decision in the group setting), and the influence of high-risk takers in the group-centered situation. The risky shift phenomenon is real and the most critical element seems to be discussion.
4. *The need to discover ways to promote group interaction, to set group goals, to learn organizational skills in group development, to learn the nature of "groupness," and generally, the realm of group experiences that promote success or failure.*
5. *The need to be sensitive to the physical environments of groups—seating arrangement preferences for maximum interaction and leadership.*
6. *The need to be aware of the factors affecting group cohesiveness—the sense of togetherness that leads to satisfactory conclusions that members can live with whether the conclusion is actually correct or not.*
7. *The need to be aware of group structure—the characteristics, environments, status, role, and norms established as a group grows from immaturity to maturity in the group process.*
8. *The need to know and understand the nature of leadership and followership and the variety of contextual situations in which group members function in a leader-related process.*
9. *The need to be sensitive to the nature of a group's goals and the subsequent success and failure rate of group tasks.*

The impression we want to leave with you is that there is a fine line between a group member's personal goals and communication abilities outside of a group setting and group-related goals and communication abilities. The ways of developing communication competencies in the group, as broadly suggested in the previous list, can remain vague and lacking in concrete suggestions for your needs unless techniques and guidelines are provided.

In that regard, Gulley and Leathers have developed an excellent test for making judgments about the value of certain communication techniques for dealing with communication problems in small groups. In particular, you should be able to apply, in these exercises, some of the concepts and guidelines for competency in group communication presented so far in this chapter. We believe that you will find the Techniques Test gives special emphasis to:

1. Dealing with the reticent or "abstract" member—#1, #3.
2. Reading nonverbal behavior—#4.
3. Indentifying and understanding other group members—#5.
4. Showing empathy toward the ego-involved member—#7.
5. Listening to and controlling conflict—#6, #9.
6. Dealing with a lack of information and an abundance of assumptions—#2.

In the Techniques Test that follows, you are to rank order the five possible techniques for each communication problem, giving a 1 to the best technique and a 5 to the worst. We would suggest that the best way to respond to the test is to complete the nine communication problems silently and then work to reach a consensus judgment in your class–laboratory group.

Techniques Test

Communication Problem 1

You are in a group where one of the group members continues to use extremely abstract language ("I believe our chief com-

The Nature of Interpersonal and Group Communication 83

petitor suffers from a cognitive occlusion"). In dealing with this communication problem, you should:

___1. Disregard the discussant's abstract language to avoid conflict.
___2. Ask the discussant if he or she has ever experienced a cognitive occlusion.
___3. Attempt to eliminate such abstractions by negatively reinforcing the discussant who uses them.
___4. Ask the discussant to define what he or she means by providing a concrete example.
___5. Hand the offending discussant a dictionary.

Communication Problem 2

At least one of the group members insists on expressing his or her views indirectly through implicit inferences ("Well, it seems to me that the question of whether we should do business with Farquardt becomes more complicated when you know where he lives"). In dealing with this communication problem, you should:

___1. Drive out to see where Farquardt lives.
___2. Wait until after the discussion and check this line of reasoning to see if it is valid.
___3. Ask the discussant to state what assumptions he or she is making about Farquardt.
___4. Try to exert group pressure to sharpen the discussant's thinking.
___5. Positively reinforce those discussants who do make their assumptions explicit.

Communication Problem 3

One of the group members insists on making statements that he or she probably thinks are humorous ("Certainly I am not suggesting that Johnson dyes his hair—it is just turning orange naturally"). In dealing with this communication problem, you should:

_____1. Question the discussant about the intent of his or her statement.
_____2. Treat yourself to a real belly laugh.
_____3. Give the discussant a copy of *Mad* magazine.
_____4. Ask yourself whether the comment is relevant.
_____5. Try to move the discussion immediately back to the task at hand.

Communication Problem 4

Lather consistently expresses himself in an incongruent manner. He often yawns while telling group members how utterly absorbing he finds the discussion to be. At other times, he gets a totally confused look on his face while assuring one of the group members that the meaning of their contribution is very clear. In dealing with this communication problem, you should:

_____1. Disregard Lather.
_____2. Accuse him of being insincere.
_____3. Flash Lather a confused expression.
_____4. Wait for five minutes before seeking clarification.
_____5. Rely on the nonverbal content of Lather's contribution as the true indicator of his meaning.

Communication Problem 5

Gordy Lather has a much higher ascribed status than any other member of the group. He makes no attempt to identify with the other members of the group, and the great differences in status are making for ineffective and inefficient communication. In dealing with this communication problem, you should:

_____1. Attempt to elevate the status of other group members with premeditated compliments.
_____2. Make it so unpleasant for Lather that he withdraws from the group.
_____3. Suggest that group members engage in role playing to illustrate the effects of a status differential.

The Nature of Interpersonal and Group Communication

____4. Work to increase your achieved status as a counterbalancing force against Lather's high ascribed status.
____5. Make Lather the group leader.

Communication Problem 6

Gordy Lather exhibits the characteristics of a closed mind; he is highly dogmatic. He is absolutely convinced of the correctness of his own opinions, absolutely rejects all opposing opinions, and lumps together all of his opponents as light thinkers. In dealing with this communication problem, you should

____1. Devote five separate group sessions to sensitivity training in order to open up Lather's mind.
____2. Suggest pointedly that some group members are becoming dogmatic.
____3. Have group members remind Lather that much of his thinking is deviant.
____4. Have all members take the Dogmatism Test and discuss the implications of their scores.
____5. Try to ostracize Lather because he is a troublemaker.

Communication Problem 7

One member of your group seems highly ego involved on one of the peripheral issues the group is discussing. Not only is this member strongly committed to his or her own position on the issue, he or she consistently rejects all alternatives that group members present. In dealing with this communication problem, you should:

____1. Suggest that the discussant join an extremist group.
____2. Make your opposition to his or her views explicit so that the discussion can zero in on the issues.
____3. Discuss central issues before moving on to the peripheral issue.
____4. Ask the discussant for some facts.
____5. Recess the meeting.

Communication Problem 8

This group seems to be experiencing the "groupthink" phenomenon. The group is very cohesive, and strong uniformity pressures exist. As a result, group members are not appraising ideas critically but simply accepting anything the leader likes. In dealing with this communication problem, you should:

____1. Call in an objective consultant who will lead the group in a vigorous discussion of those intragroup forces that are inhibiting critical thinking in the group.
____2. Add a "devil's advocate" to the group who will force members to defend their positions.
____3. Change leaders.
____4. Ostracize the "yes-men" in the group.
____5. Change the seating arrangement.

Communication Problem 9

This group is experiencing destructive conflict. Two of the members are locked in a leadership struggle, and members are beginning to choose sides. Because of the level of conflict, the group is producing few ideas, and communication has virtually ceased. In dealing with this communication problem, you should:

____1. Take a cold shower.
____2. Ride out the storm.
____3. Suggest that "nominal grouping" be used.
____4. Suggest that the group choose a leader.
____5. Move immediately to get more information that is relevant to the group's task.

Scoring the test is simple. Begin by checking the proper ranking for each communication problem (see keyed answers, which follow shortly). Compare your rankings with the keyed ranking for each communication problem. Then compute a "difference score" for each set of rankings. If your ranking deviated from

The Nature of Interpersonal and Group Communication

the keyed ranking by over one point, multiply the difference by two. For example, note how the scores for communication problem 1 would be computed.

Key Ranking	Your Ranking	Difference
3	3	0
4	4	0
2	5	6
1	2	1
5	1	8
	Total Points	= 15

Add up your computed scores for each of the nine communication problems to determine your total score on the test.

A perfect score on the Techniques Test for Resolving Small-Group Communication Problems would be 0. The higher your point total, the lower the quality of your performance on the test. Although we are still gathering data on expected performance on the test, you may use the following guidelines as a rule of thumb. If you got 40 or below, your performance was average; and above 50, your performance was poor.

Although we present and examine a variety of evaluation and assessment systems in Chapter 7, it is timely and appropriate here to examine two particular report forms that emphasizes competency in group communication. Tubb's group evaluation forms deal with the wide range of success and/or failure in decision-making procedures, group interaction, and member participation as discussed earlier. In each section you are provided the normal range of possibilities for perceiving and understanding your position in your group's structured activities. As you participate in assigned discussions in and out of class, you can broadly assess your awareness of and progress in the development of your competence in group communication behaviors.

In the checklist that follows, a range of actual procedures used for making decisions during group meetings is listed, with the sense of *consensus* at the top and *plop* (no response or action from the group) on the bottom. Depending on the communication environment, the desire for personal dominance may affect the decision-making climate of your group. Check the actual procedures used for making decisions during your meetings to see how the group fared as to topic selections, topic shift, procedures for discussion, and so on.

Decision-Making Procedures Checklist

8. Thought and feeling consensus (unanimity).
7. Near consensus (either with reservation, "I'll reluctantly go along," or dissent of one or two).
6. Majority support (a few more than half give support).
5. Minority support (a few less than half give support).
4. Teaming up (support of two or so members leads to action).
3. Topic jumping (shifting of topic without explicit deliberation and decision).
2. Railroading (one person initiates, and action follows by lack of opposition).
1. Plop (suggestion failed to get any response or action from the group).

In terms of interaction among the members of your group in various assignments or any one specific discussion assignment, there are a number of postdiscussion questions to be answered. We have included Bale's Interaction Process Analysis (see Ch. 8 of Tubbs) where you check under "Best" the three items that were done most effectively and under "Poorest" the three roles that were done least effectively. Now, you try it.

	Best	*Poorest*
1. Initiating proposals		
2. Giving information		
3. Asking for information		
4. Giving opinion		
5. Asking for opinion		
6. Elaborating		
7. Orienting toward goals		
8. Summarizing		

The Nature of Interpersonal and Group Communication

9. Harmonizing
10. Compromising
11. Gate-keeping
12. Standard-setting
13. Giving process feedback
14. Suggesting procedure
15. Clarifying

Which one (or more) of the foregoing functional roles would you particularly wish to develop skill in?

Of course, these evaluation forms are to be used for *post*discussion situational-evaluational purposes, but once used, they become checks for you to be aware of and use and/or avoid in subsequent discussions. It is still true that "experience is the best teacher" and we are most concerned that you develop your interaction skills or competencies in the discussion arena of a real group problem.

Phases in Integrated Problem Solving (PIPS)

To combine all of our efforts in this chapter to discuss interpersonal and group communication competencies and our attempts to deal with group process issues, we offer an experiential learning approach to problem solving that should be highly productive in increasing your skill development in group discussion.

Developed by Morris and Sashkin, *Phases in Integrated Problem Solving* (PIPS) provides a simple sequential task structure by which interpersonal communication competencies can be blended and developed into group communication competencies. PIPS focuses on *task* and *process* at each level, insuring a relatively high level of attention to matters of a personal, interactive nature and a personal as well as group motivational nature. PIPS provides for the breadth of a theory of group communication that recognizes many views of what is going on in a problem-solving situation as well as what motivates members and groups to work together.

The sequence of problem-solving steps in PIPS is detailed in six phases:

Phase	Activities
I Problem Definition	Explaining the problem situation, generating information, clarifying, and defining the problem.
II Problem-Solution Generation	Brainstorming solution alternatives; reviewing, revising, elaborating, and recombining solution ideas.
III Ideas to Actions	Evaluating alternatives, examining probable effects and comparing them with desired outcomes; revising ideas; developing a list of final action alternatives and selecting one for trial.
IV Solution-Action Planning	Preparing a list of action steps, with the names of persons who will be responsible for each step; developing a coordination plan.
V Solution-Evaluation Planning	Reviewing desired outcomes and development of measures of effectiveness; creating a monitoring plan for gathering evaluation data as the solution is put into action; developing contingency plans; assigning responsibilities.
VI Evaluation of the Product and the Process	Assembling evaluation data to determine the effects of actions and the effectiveness of the group's problem-solving process.

Group discussions, you can be sure, do not proceed so neatly. Morris's and Sashkin's PIPS guide you through a number of group-process issues with a series of "key questions." For each of the six problem-solving phases, five process questions and five problem-solving task activities are presented. The critical point is that your group deal with all of the issues—task and process—in each phase before moving on to the next problem-solving phases.

Each of the six phases in PIPS is introduced with a question designed to insure that everyone is aware of the focus of the phase. Similarly, each phase concludes with "publication" of the product, a written, shared activity ensuring that all group members agree on what is decided.

PIPS is designed, as mentioned earlier, to be used *during*

group problem solving. Not everyone in your group needs to use PIPS during a discussion, however. One person can watch the task items while another can watch process items.

Unlike most questionnaires, it does not ask for ideas or opinions; each question identifies an important step that must occur for effective problem solving to come about. On the left-hand side of each page are questions that review *what* should happen (tasks). On the right, coordinated with each task question, is a process question, reviewing *how* the task should be done.

If at any time you feel that a step is being left out or improperly performed, interrupt whatever discussion is taking place and bring your observation to the attention of all group members. To use the instrument, each group member reads each question in turn and rates the group on that item. If anyone rates the group below "5" ("this step was *fully* accomplished"), the group as a whole reviews that step. Only when everyone agrees that the step was *fully* accomplished does the group move on to the following step.

Doing this is not as complicated as it might sound at first. You will have to look at only *one* page—thirteen questions—at any one time, and the questions are in sequence. That is, the activity described in question 2 should occur *before* the group attempts to respond to question 3.

You might also think that going through each step and taking the discussion time needed to do so will be a lengthy process. However, although the group will probably take more time than usual to solve a problem, the extra time will *not* be a great deal. And, if prior group discussions have been *extremely* poor, you might actually find that this procedure *saves* time. In any case, as the group gets better at solving problems and eventually dispenses with this tool, the time required will diminish and there will also be a clear payoff in effective, quickly implemented solutions.

Each of the six phases follows a basic problem-solving format:

Phase I: *Problem Definition.* Often we assume that we know what the problem is, but just as often we are wrong and are looking only at a symptom or, at best, only part of the problem. The questions in Phase I are designed to guide the group in fully exploring, clarifying, and defining the problem.

Phase II: *Problem-Solution Generation.* People tend to be solution minded, rather than problem oriented. Phase II is designed to prolong the idea-generating process and prevent premature decisions. Although often the solution we choose is the first or one of the first suggested, research has shown very clearly that solutions can be greatly improved by examining as many alternatives as possible. The more ideas we consider, the more likely we are to come up with a greater number of *good* ideas.

Phase III: *Ideas to Actions.* Now the group is ready to evaluate the ideas and come up with a final solution. Even though an idea may not work alone, it may have a good "part"; time can be taken to combine these good parts of various ideas and even to classify solution ideas into "sets." Each alternative can then be carefully, critically evaluated. People will be more able to help and participate if they do not feel attacked or threatened; rather than weeding out poor alternatives (and making those who suggested them feel defensive), it is better to select the *best* ones and concentrate on those until everyone can agree on one or two solutions.

Phase IV: *Solution-Action Planning.* There is now a solution to try out, and the chances are that it will work more smoothly if the actions needed to put it into operation are carefully planned. This means looking for problems in advance, planning to involve those persons whose support will be needed, and assigning and accepting action responsibilities. Only if the group determines *who* is to do *what* and *when* can the solution have a fair test.

Phase V: *Solution-Evaluation Planning.* Unfortunately, most groups stop at Phase IV, losing the chance to learn from experience. Even if a solution is a tremendous success, it is useful to know exactly what it was about the actions taken that made the solution work so well. It can then be repeated more easily. If a solution is a total disaster, we may feel like hiding the fact that we had anything to do with it. But it is necessary to know *exactly* what went wrong so that the same things can be avoided in the future. Of course, in real life, solutions generally work moderately well; they are neither spectacular successes nor spectacular failures. Keeping track of exactly what is happening allows minor improvements or adjustments that will help significantly in solving the problem. This is best done not by guesswork or trial and error, but on the basis of hard, accurate information about the effects of actions. This phase offers the greatest potential for learning to solve problems. Again, *what* kind of evaluation information is needed, *who* will obtain it, and *when* must be specified.

Phase VI: *Evaluation of the Product and the Process.* When the "votes are all in," when there is enough information to evaluate how well and to what degree the solution worked, it is time for another group meeting, for final evaluation. At this point it is possible to see what the outcomes were and whether the problem was solved. If the problem or some part of it remains, the group can "recycle"—look at the information it has, perhaps even redefine the problem, and come up with new ideas or try out a previously chosen alternative. It will be necessary to repeat the steps in Phases III to V. If the problem *was* solved, it is important to consider what actions are necessary to keep it from reappearing. This is also the time to review and evaluate how well the group worked together.

The key to using the problem-solving procedure detailed here is to follow each step in each phase to the point at which everyone can agree that the step—and phase—is *fully* accomplished. As you use PIPS in your classroom discussions, we believe that you will find, with your instructor's assistance, that a seemingly "idealistic" approach to problem solving can work if you have the needed interaction-process skills.

Finally, the PIPS model can lead to an internalized sense of accomplishing minimal and maximal tasks as a competent group member. Surely, the argument is clear now that the measuring rods of success in effective group communication skills center around effective group behavior that leads to task and process success.

Phase I. Problem Definition: Exploring, Clarifying, Defining

To What Extent Has the Step Been Accomplished?

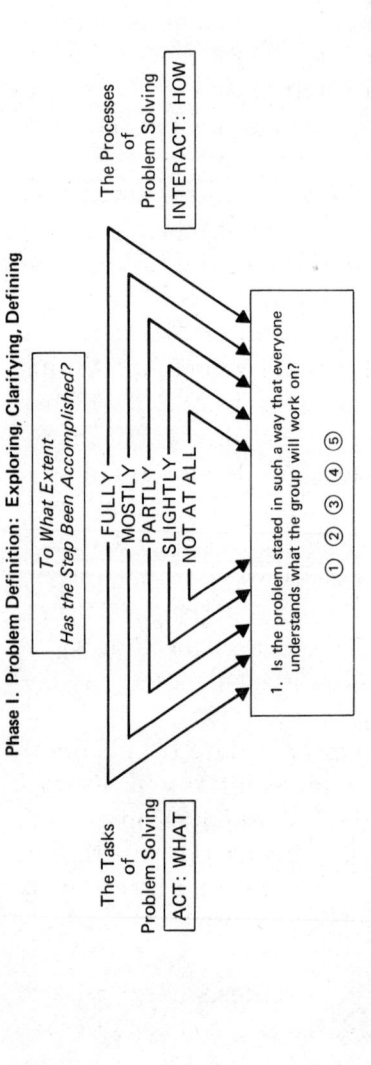

The Tasks of Problem Solving
ACT: WHAT

FULLY
MOSTLY
PARTLY
SLIGHTLY
NOT AT ALL

① ② ③ ④ ⑤

The Processes of Problem Solving
INTERACT: HOW

1. Is the problem stated in such a way that everyone understands what the group will work on?

2. To what extent have information resources been sought out? Is everyone who might have relevant data present or represented at the meeting?*
   5 4 3 2 1

3. Is all of the available information about the problem brought to light and discussed?*
   5 4 3 2 1

4. Is the group taking the information relating to the stated problem and considering how it all "fits together"?
   5 4 3 2 1

5. Is there consideration of what the situation would be like if the problem were solved?
   5 4 3 2 1

6. Has the problem finally been stated in a way such that everyone understands and agrees to a common problem definition?
   5 4 3 2 1

2. Are those persons most directly involved in the problem encouraged by the leader and group members to participate in giving information?
   1 2 3 4 5

3. Is there an "atmosphere" that encourages openness and sharing? Do all group members feel free to speak?
   1 2 3 4 5

4. Are all persons encouraged to make suggestions about how the information fits together to define the problem?
   1 2 3 4 5

5. Are group members keeping the discussion problem centered, avoiding consideration of solution alternatives?
   1 2 3 4 5

6. Has every person been asked about his or her agreement with the final problem statement as written and posted?
   1 2 3 4 5

Record in detail the final problem statement on a separate sheet of paper.

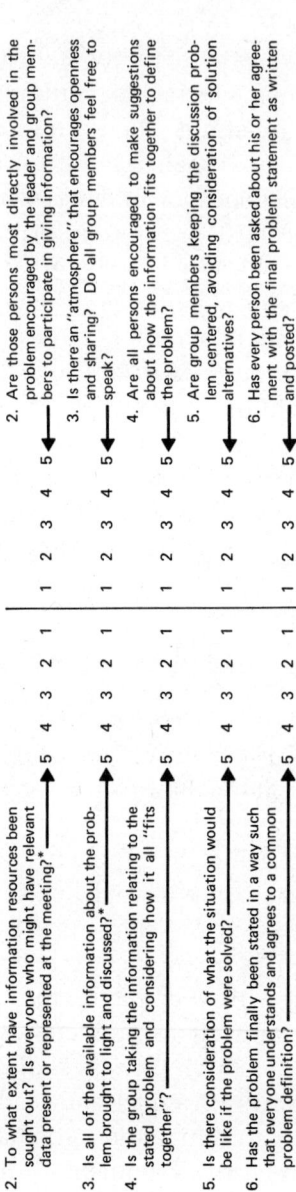

Reproduced by permission from ORGANIZATION BEHAVIOR IN ACTION by Morris and Sashkin, copyright © 1976, West Publishing Company.
*If additional information is found to be necessary, it should be obtained before going further with the discussion.

FIGURE 4-1.

94

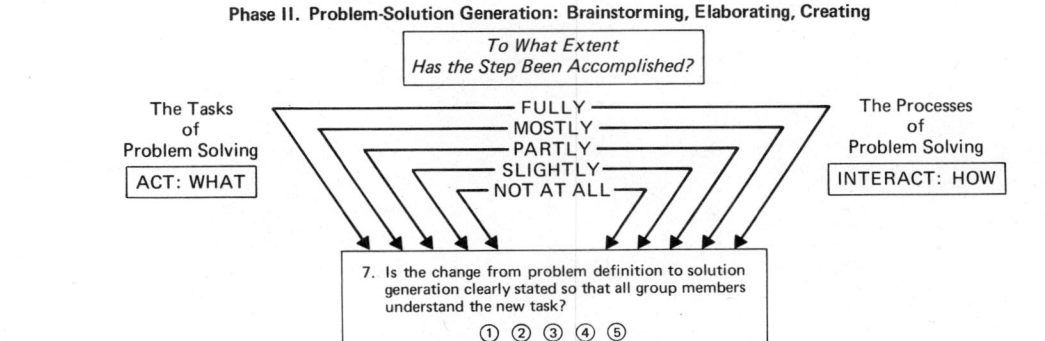

Phase II. Problem-Solution Generation: Brainstorming, Elaborating, Creating

The Tasks of Problem Solving
ACT: WHAT

To What Extent Has the Step Been Accomplished?

FULLY
MOSTLY
PARTLY
SLIGHTLY
NOT AT ALL
① ② ③ ④ ⑤

The Processes of Problem Solving
INTERACT: HOW

7. Is the change from problem definition to solution generation clearly stated so that all group members understand the new task?

8. Have the rules of brainstorming (all ideas accepted and posted; no criticism; repetition and "piggy-backing" on other ideas OK) been reviewed and posted before beginning? 5 4 3 2 1

9. Are as many ideas generated as possible, using all the resources of the group? 5 4 3 2 1

10. When all ideas are out, is the list reviewed in detail, clarifying items when necessary and expanding or adding to the ideas generated? 5 4 3 2 1

11. Is the group taking time to examine the list and combine various ideas into "sets" of alternatives? 5 4 3 2 1

12. Has the group developed a list of at least several clearly stated alternatives? 5 4 3 2 1

8. Are the leader or other group members taking time to encourage those who might be slower at giving out ideas, pausing and asking for more ideas when necessary? 1 2 3 4 5

9. Are all ideas recognized and welcomed regardless of their content (e.g., including even ideas that seem "foolish")? 1 2 3 4 5

10. Is criticism tactfully discouraged and are evaluative comments postponed (e.g., asking for another alternative instead of criticism)? 1 2 3 4 5

11. Is the group able to prevent any one member from dominating the discussion or imposing his/her frame of reference on the group? 1 2 3 4 5

12. Have all final alternatives been posted (on chalkboard or newsprint) for everyone to see? 1 2 3 4 5

Record the list of solution alternatives on a separate sheet of paper.

FIGURE 4-2.

Phase III. Ideas to Actions: Evaluating, Combining, Selecting

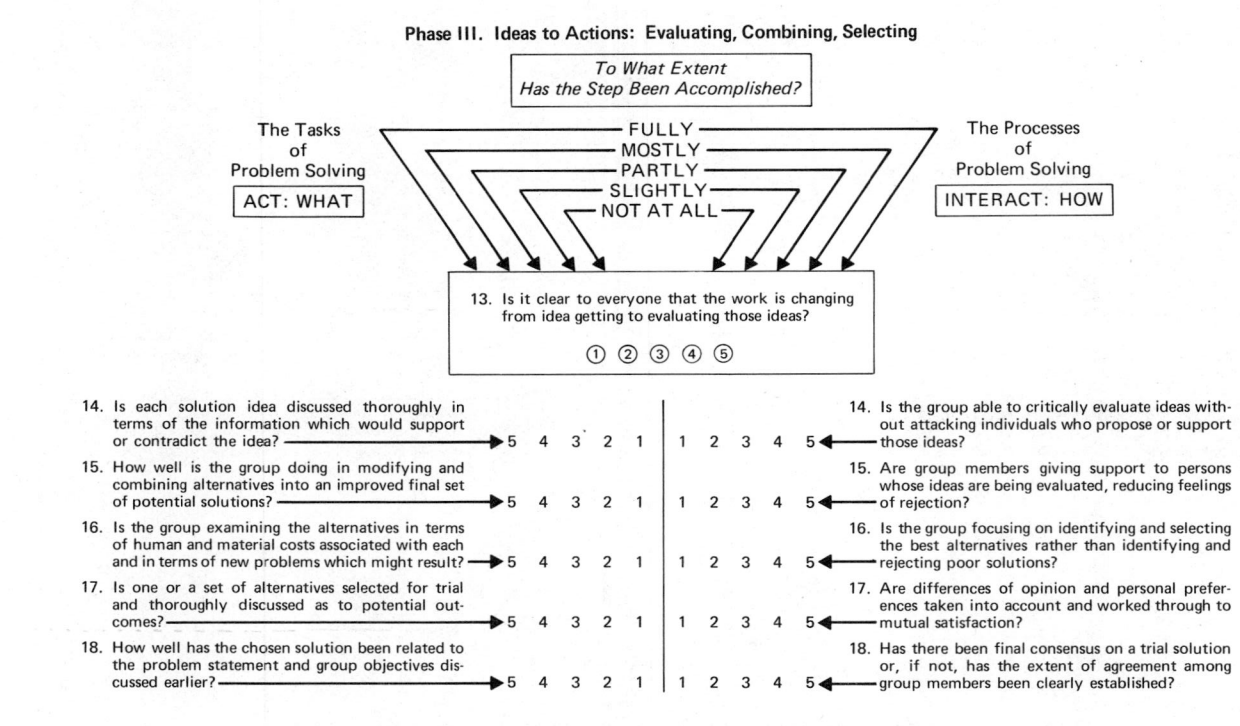

To What Extent Has the Step Been Accomplished?

The Tasks of Problem Solving
ACT: WHAT

The Processes of Problem Solving
INTERACT: HOW

FULLY
MOSTLY
PARTLY
SLIGHTLY
NOT AT ALL

13. Is it clear to everyone that the work is changing from idea getting to evaluating those ideas?

① ② ③ ④ ⑤

14. Is each solution idea discussed thoroughly in terms of the information which would support or contradict the idea?   5 4 3 2 1

15. How well is the group doing in modifying and combining alternatives into an improved final set of potential solutions?   5 4 3 2 1

16. Is the group examining the alternatives in terms of human and material costs associated with each and in terms of new problems which might result?   5 4 3 2 1

17. Is one or a set of alternatives selected for trial and thoroughly discussed as to potential outcomes?   5 4 3 2 1

18. How well has the chosen solution been related to the problem statement and group objectives discussed earlier?   5 4 3 2 1

14. Is the group able to critically evaluate ideas without attacking individuals who propose or support those ideas?   1 2 3 4 5

15. Are group members giving support to persons whose ideas are being evaluated, reducing feelings of rejection?   1 2 3 4 5

16. Is the group focusing on identifying and selecting the best alternatives rather than identifying and rejecting poor solutions?   1 2 3 4 5

17. Are differences of opinion and personal preferences taken into account and worked through to mutual satisfaction?   1 2 3 4 5

18. Has there been final consensus on a trial solution or, if not, has the extent of agreement among group members been clearly established?   1 2 3 4 5

Record in detail the final trial solution on a separate sheet of paper.

FIGURE 4-3.

Phase IV. Solution-Action Planning: Planning, Assigning, Coordinating

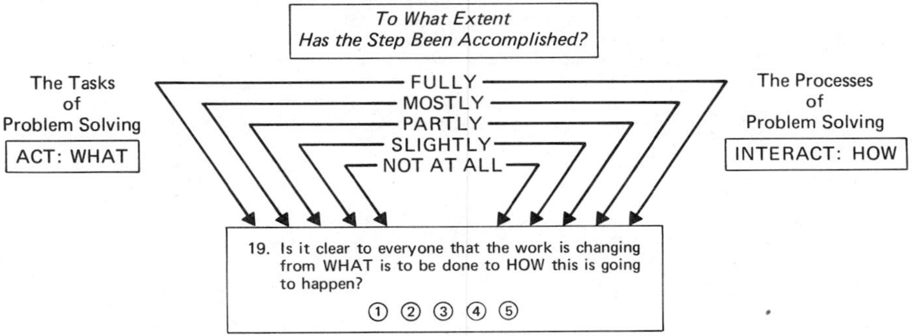

*To What Extent
Has the Step Been Accomplished?*

— FULLY
— MOSTLY
— PARTLY
— SLIGHTLY
— NOT AT ALL

The Tasks
of
Problem Solving
ACT: WHAT

The Processes
of
Problem Solving
INTERACT: HOW

19. Is it clear to everyone that the work is changing from WHAT is to be done to HOW this is going to happen?
① ② ③ ④ ⑤

20. Is the group preparing a list of sequenced action steps which will be needed to implement the solution, including a realistic time schedule?
5 4 3 2 1

21. Is the group able to identify and list various forces which might help or hinder the action process being planned?
5 4 3 2 1

22. Are all of the needed resources (material as well as human, and including persons not present) for accomplishing each of the action steps being clearly identified?
5 4 3 2 1

23. Is the group able to clearly assign responsibilities for carrying out specific action steps and for coordinating that process?
5 4 3 2 1

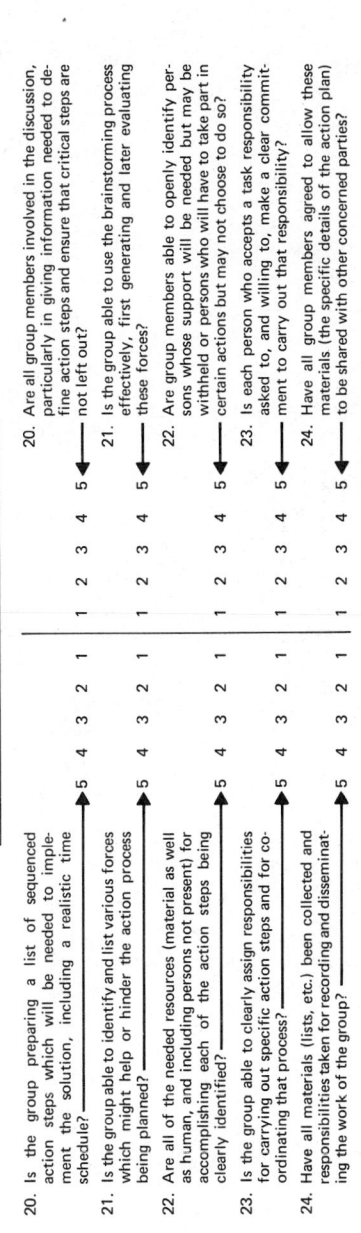

24. Have all materials (lists, etc.) been collected and responsibilities taken for recording and disseminating the work of the group?
5 4 3 2 1

20. Are all group members involved in the discussion, particularly in giving information needed to define action steps and ensure that critical steps are not left out?
1 2 3 4 5

21. Is the group able to use the brainstorming process effectively, first generating and later evaluating these forces?
1 2 3 4 5

22. Are group members able to openly identify persons whose support will be needed but may be withheld or persons who will have to take part in certain actions but may not choose to do so?
1 2 3 4 5

23. Is each person who accepts a task responsibility asked to, and willing to, make a clear commitment to carry out that responsibility?
1 2 3 4 5

24. Have all group members agreed to allow these materials (the specific details of the action plan) to be shared with other concerned parties?
1 2 3 4 5

Record on a separate sheet of paper the sequence of action steps agreed to, who accepted responsibility for each step, and the time schedule for actions.

FIGURE 4-4.

Phase V. Solution-Evaluation Planning: Describing, Monitoring, Contingency Planning

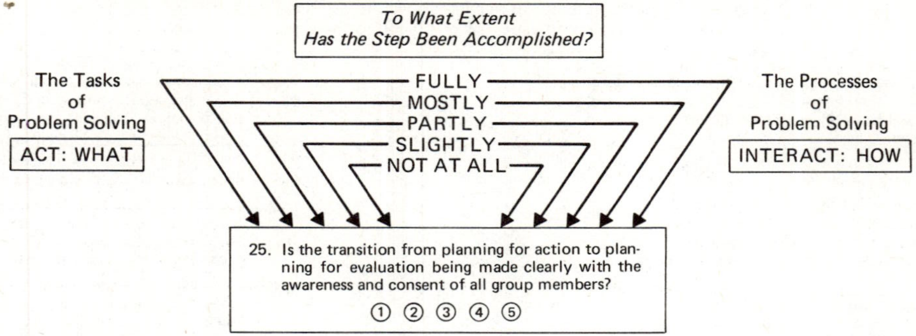

The Tasks of Problem Solving
ACT: WHAT

To What Extent Has the Step Been Accomplished?

FULLY
MOSTLY
PARTLY
SLIGHTLY
NOT AT ALL

The Processes of Problem Solving
INTERACT: HOW

25. Is the transition from planning for action to planning for evaluation being made clearly with the awareness and consent of all group members?
① ② ③ ④ ⑤

26. Is the group reviewing the desired solution outcomes and developing measures for each action step, which would indicate the degree of success in attaining the outcomes?
5 4 3 2 1

27. Is a timetable developed for step-by-step interim evaluation (monitoring of effects as action plans are implemented)?
5 4 3 2 1

28. Are responsibilities clearly assigned for gathering evaluation data and preparing reports?
5 4 3 2 1

29. Are contingency plans outlined for critical steps (such that the overall plan could continue with modification but without major interruption)?
5 4 3 2 1

30. Have plans been made for dissemination of interim results, and has a final evaluation meeting date been set?
5 4 3 2 1

26. Are any differences among group members regarding definitions and measures of success openly discussed, explored, and resolved?
1 2 3 4 5

27. Are group members free in expressing concern or support for the details of the time schedule?
1 2 3 4 5

28. Do the persons accepting these responsibilities express clear commitment to their accomplishment?
1 2 3 4 5

29. Are all group members involved in giving ideas for meeting such contingencies (particularly, those who have action responsibilities for the critical steps)?
1 2 3 4 5

30. Has everyone agreed to these plans and the data; have any reservations been openly expressed and resolved?
1 2 3 4 5

Record on a separate sheet of paper the solution-evaluation criteria, the specific evaluation plan (actions, timetable, and responsibilities) and the final evaluation meeting date.

FIGURE 4-5.

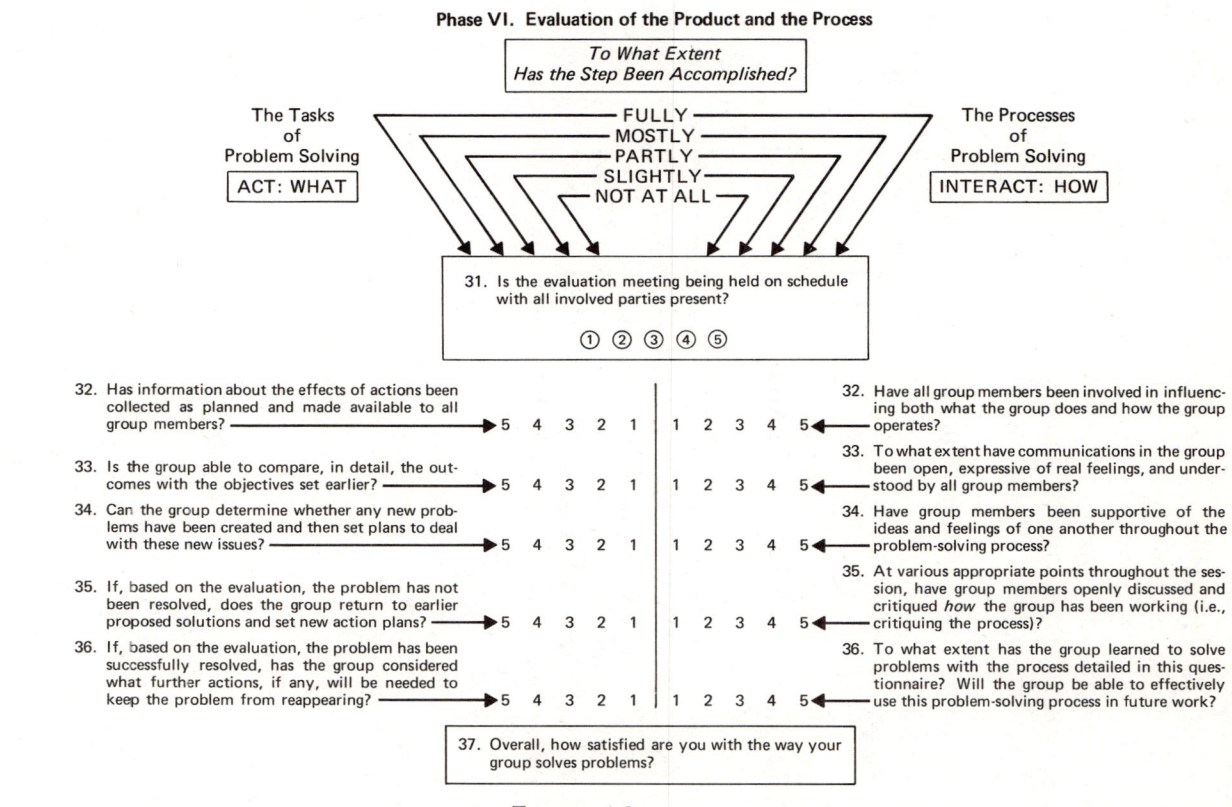

Phase VI. Evaluation of the Product and the Process

To What Extent Has the Step Been Accomplished?

The Tasks of Problem Solving
ACT: WHAT

FULLY — MOSTLY — PARTLY — SLIGHTLY — NOT AT ALL

The Processes of Problem Solving
INTERACT: HOW

31. Is the evaluation meeting being held on schedule with all involved parties present?

① ② ③ ④ ⑤

32. Has information about the effects of actions been collected as planned and made available to all group members?
5 4 3 2 1 — 1 2 3 4 5
32. Have all group members been involved in influencing both what the group does and how the group operates?

33. Is the group able to compare, in detail, the outcomes with the objectives set earlier?
5 4 3 2 1 — 1 2 3 4 5
33. To what extent have communications in the group been open, expressive of real feelings, and understood by all group members?

34. Can the group determine whether any new problems have been created and then set plans to deal with these new issues?
5 4 3 2 1 — 1 2 3 4 5
34. Have group members been supportive of the ideas and feelings of one another throughout the problem-solving process?

35. If, based on the evaluation, the problem has not been resolved, does the group return to earlier proposed solutions and set new action plans?
5 4 3 2 1 — 1 2 3 4 5
35. At various appropriate points throughout the session, have group members openly discussed and critiqued *how* the group has been working (i.e., critiquing the process)?

36. If, based on the evaluation, the problem has been successfully resolved, has the group considered what further actions, if any, will be needed to keep the problem from reappearing?
5 4 3 2 1 — 1 2 3 4 5
36. To what extent has the group learned to solve problems with the process detailed in this questionnaire? Will the group be able to effectively use this problem-solving process in future work?

37. Overall, how satisfied are you with the way your group solves problems?

FIGURE 4-6.

Summary

We have come some distance in this chapter from describing the nature of interpersonal skills that you should be aware of to the nature of group communication skills that you should learn and practice in the classroom. We have listed these two skills areas; suggested communication problems for you to test your awareness and competency; provided a series of postdiscussion forms focusing on competency interests; and finally, introduced you to PIPS as an instrument guide to shepherd the group as they practice the interaction-process skills so important for group problem solving.

References and Further Reading

The material relating to the interpersonal and group communication competencies can be found in two excellent studies conducted by Phillip W. Keezer, Patricia Garrighan, Susan Barry, Steven McGee, Mandy Bratton, Marcia Moore, and John Kares Smith—all members of the Project to Assess Communication Skills, Department of Communication Studies, State University of New York, Oswego, New York. To date, the PACS staff has prepared two working papers—March, 1977, and September, 1977. Related research in the area includes David W. Kale, "What is a Competency?" a paper presented to the Eastern Communication Association Convention, New York City, March, 1977; Vincent DiSalvo, David C. Larson, and William J. Seiler, "Communication Skills Needed by Persons in Business Organizations," *Communication Education*, November, 1976, 25, pp. 270–275; Carl E. Thoresen, "Oral Non-Participation in College Students," *American Educational Research Journal*, 3 (1966); James McCroskey et al., "Communication Apprehension and Self-Esteem," *Human Communication Research*, 3 (Spring, 1977), pp. 269–277; Gayle K. Levison, "The Basic Speech Communication Course: Establishing Minimal Oral Competencies and Exemption Procedures," *Communication Education* 25 (September, 1975); Gayle K. Levison and Richard Long, "Communication Competencies: A List," ECA Basic Course Conference, Competency Task Force, Boston, Mass., November 4, 1976.

BARRETT, HAROLD. *Practical Uses of Speech Communication.* New York: Holt, Rinehart and Winston, 1978, pp. 5–6, 11.

GULLEY, HALBERT E., and DALE G. LEATHERS. *Communication and Group Process: Techniques for Improving the Quality of Small-Group Communication* (3rd Ed.). New York: Holt, Rinehart and Winston, 1977, pp. 146–151.

PFEIFFER, J. WILLIAM and JOHN E. JONES (Eds.). The 1978 Annual Handbook for Group Facilitators, La Jolla, Calif.: University Associates, 1978. Used with permission.

SHAW, MARVIN. *Group Dynamics: The Psychology of Small Group Behavior* (2nd Ed.). New York: McGraw-Hill Book Co., 1976, pp. 60–61.

TUBBS, STEWART. *A Systems Approach to Small Group Interaction* (Instructor's Manual). Reading, Mass.: Addison-Wesley, 1978, pp. 26–27, 30.

Nonverbal Dimensions of Group Communication

OBJECTIVES:
After studying this chapter, you should be better able to:

Understand the role of nonverbal communication in discussion.

Define nonverbal communication.

Appreciate the value of nonverbal communication in discussion.

Identify and describe the systems of nonverbal communication.

Identify and describe the interrelationship of the various systems with each other and with verbal communication.

Attempt to use and interpret nonverbal communication in its context.

5

FUNDAMENTALS OF GROUP COMMUNICATION[1]

GENERAL KNOWLEDGE ABOUT GROUP COMMUNICATION

1. Nature/Usefulness
2. Types/Format
3. The Process and Its Phases
4. Strengths/Weaknesses

→

TASK DIMENSION

1. Planning/Preparation
2. Procedures/Arrangements
3. Interpersonal/Group Communication Competencies
4. Phases of Integrated Problem Solving
5. Leadership Responsibilities

→

SOCIAL DIMENSION

1. Self/Group Characteristics
2. Self/Group Concepts
3. Interpersonal/Group Attraction
4. Social Attributes
5. **Dimensions of Nonverbal Behavior**
6. Leadership Characteristics
7. Role/Status/Power
8. Mature/Immature Group Characteristics

→

ASSESSMENT

1. Formative/Summative
2. Individual/Group Evaluation Technique
3. Maturing Member/Group: Strengths and Weaknesses

[1] Concepts in bold face are emphasized in this chapter.

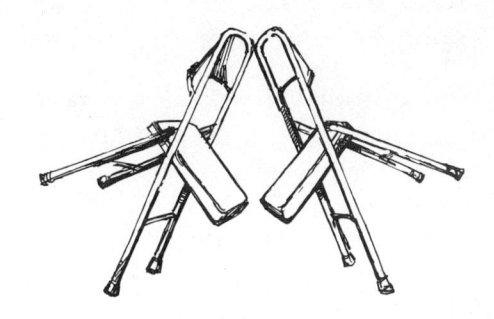

Nonverbal communication plays a crucial role in human interaction. Interest in nonverbal communication has increased substantially in recent years, and yet many works on communication make no reference to it. We continue to make the word "communication" synonymous with linguistic interchange. Even in this text our emphasis is overwhelmingly on linguistic aspects with only one chapter dealing with nonverbal communication.

Several books on aspects of nonverbal communication have achieved considerable popularity in the past ten years. Julius Fast in *Body Language* (1970) provides explicit descriptions of bodily actions and suggestions for interpretation of what such actions mean. John Molloy's *Dress for Success* (1975) is an interesting and provocative book that presents to the layman the results of "empirical research" dealing with matters of dress as it relates to effective nonverbal communication. Nierenberg and Calero (1971) have written *How to Read People Like a Book*. Some of the popular writing has perhaps rushed to conclusions about the meaning of some nonverbal signals, and have perhaps been overly optimistic about the prescriptive value of nonverbal communication.

However, intensive research by linguists, anthropologists, psychiatrists, and others has begun to produce an identifiable area of study. Just as linguistic communication had been dissected and described in a highly complex system, so too were researchers developing a very comprehensive description of the organizational schematic of nonverbal communication and volumes of research reports to support nearly unbelievable detail of description in nonverbal communication. Birdwhistle (1970) exemplifies this detail when he claims that "the human face alone is capable of making some 250,000 different expressions. I have fifteen placement symbols plus eleven special markers sufficient to record the significant positions of all the faces I have ever seen. Less than one hundred symbols are all that are required to deal with any kinesic subject which I have yet studied. . . ."

The basic communication model shown in Figure 5-1 represents how we transmit information or ideas through normal linguistic communication, whether written or oral. This same model, as shown in Figure 5-2, can also demonstrate how we communicate nonverbally from source (signaller) to the ultimate destination (receiver), a process described by Argyle (1975).

At this stage you may be asking, "Could you define nonverbal communication?" There is so much included in nonverbal communication that it is difficult to give just one definition. As you will see later in this chapter, there really are many nonverbal systems at work and each can be separately defined. However, a general definition of nonverbal communication can be given by telling you what it is not. Eisenberg and Smith (1971) offer the following: "*All communication except that which is coded in words is generally referred to as nonverbal communication.*"

Let us examine some of the major differences between linguistic or verbal communication and nonverbal communication. First, in verbal communication you can choose whether you will speak or not; you can control your communication in that way. In nonverbal communication, if you are in the presence of others you have no choice but to communicate. Involuntarily or voluntarily you will be communicating.

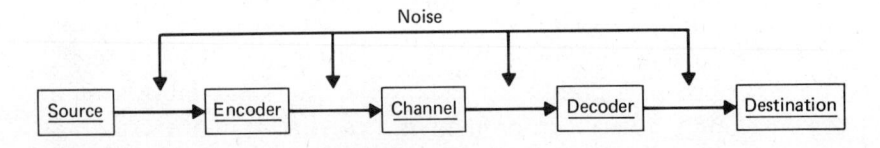

```
                              Noise
              ┌───────┬─────────┬─────────┐
              ▼       ▼         ▼         ▼
 ┌────────┐  ┌─────────┐  ┌─────────┐  ┌─────────┐  ┌─────────────┐
 │ Source │→ │ Encoder │→ │ Channel │→ │ Decoder │→ │ Destination │
 └────────┘  └─────────┘  └─────────┘  └─────────┘  └─────────────┘
```

Source: The speaker — a person with speech ability.
Encoder: Some meaning is put in linguistic form and transformed into an oral signal.
Channel: The oral signal is carried through the medium of air waves.
Decoder: The oral signal is then translated into some meaning.
Destination: The listener — a person with hearing/listening ability.

FIGURE 5-1. Oral Adaptation of Communication Model.

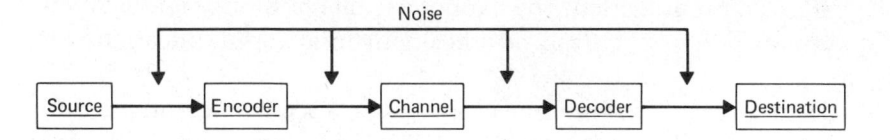

Nonverbal Dimensions of Group Communication

```
                            Noise
        ┌─────────────┬─────────────┬─────────────┐
        ▼             ▼             ▼             ▼
┌────────┐   ┌────────┐   ┌────────┐   ┌────────┐   ┌────────────┐
│ Source │──▶│Encoder │──▶│Channel │──▶│Decoder │──▶│Destination │
└────────┘   └────────┘   └────────┘   └────────┘   └────────────┘
```

Source: The signaller — a person with full control of bodily movement.
Encoder: Some meaning is translated into a nonverbal signal.
Channel: The signal is carried through the medium of light waves.
Decoder: The signal is then translated into some meaning.
Destination: The receiver — a person with visual perception ability.

FIGURE 5-2. Non-Verbal Adaptation of Communication Model.

Second, linguistic communication is more reasoned, nonverbal is more spontaneous. Sometimes we say a person talks without thinking, meaning that the person has said something that he later wishes he had not said. Our nonverbal communication tends often to have that type of spontaneity, which causes many to feel that is a more accurate reflector of our true feelings on a subject.

Third, linguistic communication is more arbitrary than nonverbal. Words have a meaning because in our language we *assign* a meaning on an arbitrary basis. A particular nonverbal communication signal may have a relatively fixed arbitrary meaning, but much nonverbal communication is not arbitrary and has no specific assigned meaning.

Fourth, verbal communication is more cognitive while nonverbal is more emotive. We use the verbal mode to discuss all levels of abstraction in great detail and to describe objects and relationships because it has precision and other characteristics that make it suitable for this communication need. The verbal mode can also communicate feeling and emotion, but nonverbal communication tends to operate more in this area because of its basic characteristics. We sometimes talk of the difficulty of putting feelings into words. We say, "Words can't express how I feel," or "I just can't tell you how much this means." On the other hand, it is difficult to keep emotive considerations out of your actions.

Another distinction is that verbal communication is self-reflexive, or you can use language to talk about language. In nonverbal communication, you cannot use one of the communication systems to describe itself or other nonverbal communication systems.

Sixth, verbal communication has a specific beginning and ending. Nonverbal communication, on the other hand, flows and may not have a recognizable beginning or ending.

And, a final distinction, nonverbal communication uses many channels and may use more than one channel at a time. Linguistic communication uses only the oral/writing channels.

We mentioned at the beginning of the chapter that nonverbal communication played an extremely important role in all human interaction. "How?" you may ask, and we will examine that question first and then look at the particular importance of nonverbal communication in the small-group setting.

Leathers (1976) identifies six major reasons why nonverbal communication is generally important for us in our society: (1) Nonverbal communication is a more significant determinant of meaning in the interpersonal context; (2) feelings and emotions are more accurately exchanged by nonverbal than verbal means; (3) deception and distortion are less evident; (4) nonverbal cues assist linguistic communication to achieve higher quality; (5) nonverbal cues are very efficient; and (6) nonverbal cues are very useful for suggestion.

A graphic demonstration of the impact of nonverbal communication resulted from a study by Mehrabian (1971). He reported finding in his research that only 7 percent of a communication was verbal, 55 percent of communication was directly related to facial expression, and 93 percent of the communication occurred through various nonverbal communication systems. Although this information seems hard to accept for the average person who equates communication with speaking, the general strength of importance of nonverbal communication has been demonstrated by other researchers as well. Birdwhistle (1970) states that "in psuedo-statistics probably no more than 30 to 35 percent of the social meaning of a conversation or interaction is carried on by words."

Nonverbal communication has particular importance in small groups because some of the special unique characteristics of nonverbal communication are very similar to or supportive of special

Nonverbal Dimensions of Group Communication

characteristics of small groups. Gulley and Leathers (1977) and Rosenfeld (1973) discuss some of these similarities in their texts on small-group communication. Let us consider four particular ways that nonverbal communication is especially helpful to small groups: (1) the variety of channels available in nonverbal communication; (2) the physical togetherness of groups; (3) the "relationship-building" that characterizes a group; and (4) the need for multiple cues in small-group communication.

In any small group only one individual should be talking at a time in the oral mode. Conversation between discussion participants that is not directed to the discussion group as a whole is discouraged. There must be order in the group to protect the group from chaos or a general "bull" session. In the nonverbal communication mode, however, virtually everyone in the discussion group *can* and *is* "talking" nonverbally *all* of the time and may be being "read" much of the time. While a discussion participant may only be able to comment orally a few times in an entire group discussion, the same individual would be communicating most of the time nonverbally. The availability of multiple senses such as sight, touch, smell to operate at the same time without interfering with the oral mode gives nonverbal communication a distinct advantage. It also places a large responsibility on each participant as nonverbal communicator (initiator of nonverbal signals) and as a receiver of the signals of others while maintaining intimate contact with the oral communication operating at the same time.

Second, small groups are physically organized for closeness in the small group communication setting. In Chapter 2 we described various physical arrangements and indicated the value of all group members being in close proximity to each other and within direct eyesight of each other. This is the type of setting in which all of the various nonverbal communication systems can work most effectively.

Third, small groups are more than a mere collection of bodies together in a room or gathered around a table. Small groups form, build, and develop interpersonally as relationships mature. The expression of feelings and attitudes is a key factor in developing effective group discussion. Again, this characteristic of a small group makes nonverbal communication particularly useful because the nonverbal communication systems tend to be expressive outlets for feelings and attitudes more so than linguistic communication. Thus, "relationship-building," which is at the heart of small-group communication, is fostered by nonverbal communication.

Fourth, when small groups meet to discuss they have a considerable need for management or regulatory tools to keep the oral discussion flowing through its process. Much of this regulation is accomplished through verbal communication when members make comments such as "What we have said, then, is . . ." (an internal symmary); or "Another point we should consider is . . ." (moving forward to another topic); or "That's a good point but I don't exactly understand how it relates to our problem" (redirecting to keep the discussion on track). However, it is not always possible to contribute regulatory oral comments because only one can speak at a time, but there are numerous nonverbal cues you can give that will express feelings such as "I don't understand," or "Let Jane speak," or "You're monopolizing the discussion."

We hope that you have a sense of the importance of nonverbal communication both in general and in its specific relation to our study of small-group communication. As Hopper (1976) has put it, "Nonverbal communication behavior is important for the same reasons that verbal communication is. It carries information that helps us predict other people's behavior and the structure of social situations so that we can behave appropriately."

Nonverbal Communication Systems

We have discussed the similarities and differences of verbal and nonverbal communication. Before we begin a detailed description of nonverbal systems, let us reemphasize that verbal and nonverbal communication are closely interrelated and frequently work cooperatively to communicate.

From the research on nonverbal communication to date, we can categorize most nonverbal communication as being a part of one of the following systems: kinesic, proxemic, artifactual, and vocalic (paralingual). Each of these systems is described for you in the following pages with particular emphasis on those that seem to have the greater direct relevance for a study of small-group communication. In that sense, the authors believe that the listing is in a general hierarchial listing as it relates to relative importance of the role each plays in small-group communication.

Kinesics

Kinesics is a study of body motion as a form of communication (Birdwhistle, 1970). It is a developing field of study in which researchers are attempting to identify and codify basic body motions, and attempting to develop better understandings of how to determine the meanings of nonverbal body motions. It is still a new area of study in behavioral science and much remains to be learned, especially about the meaning of the body motions. The research has been able to develop fairly thorough classification systems through descriptive/observational research.

Body motion is a large system and can be subdivided into the following units: facial communication, eye (gaze) communication, gestural communication, postural communication, body contact communication. In reading the following sections, you should bear in mind that the interpretation of meaning of nonverbal communication is context and culture bound. Isolating a cue or signal from its context will likely lead you to false interpretations.

Facial Communication

Argyle (1975) states that "the face is the most important area for nonverbal signalling." In a study by Zaidel and Mehrabian (1973), it was found that "the facial channel was generally more effective than the vocal channel for communicating attitude." Knapp (1972), in discussing facial expression, states that "some say it is the primary source of information next to human speech."

Surely each of us has experienced numerous settings in

which a facial expression cogently communicated a feeling to us. Whether it was a stern look from a parent, or an "I love you" look from a romantic mate, we have experienced facial expression that communicated as profoundly or more so than oral communication. The widely used simple drawings of sad/happy faces (see Fig. 5-3) indicate how the full face can communicate just how we feel inside.

In the main, facial expressions are used in three rather different ways: (1) to assess personality characteristics; (2) to assess emotions; or (3) to assist interaction linked to speech (Argyle, 1975). Much of our facial expression is taught as a part of our socialization; it is somewhat controlled by an individual, and thus facial expression is seen as a self-expression of an individual. Our emotions speak loudly through facial expression as we show surprise, scorn, pleasure, unhappiness, disappointment, elation, inquisitiveness, acceptance, rejection, and scores of other emotions, reactions, and feelings. And much of our facial expression is developed to reinforce our speech.

Gulley and Leathers (1977) adapt from Ekman and Friesen (1975) a classification of three techniques used by a message sender to alter facial expression: (1) qualifying, (2) modulating, or (3) falsifying. You qualify a facial expression when you change or alter a follow-up facial expression immediately after another facial expression with the intent to modify the first expression. For example, you may realize that your facial expression is one of extreme hurt, and wishing to modify it, change it to mere displeasure. Modulation of facial expression is an attempt to control facial expression in terms of strength or weakness, a restraint against expressing a feeling totally, openly, and accurately. Falsifying through facial expression is expressing oneself in some way other than how one really feels.

FIGURE 5-3. Sad-Happy Face.

Nonverbal Dimensions of Group Communication 113

Facial communication tends to be spontaneous and natural and will usually show your actual feelings. As the research indicates, you can control it to some extent. As a participant in discussion, you may be able to improve your interaction with your group by increasing your sensitivity to facial expression and attempting to regulate it as appropriate.

An increased awareness of facial expression and its control can also assist you in becoming a better student of facial expression. While participating in a group, you must be listening and following the oral discussion and thinking of contributions you can make. Add to these responsibilities a need for carefully observing facial expression and other nonverbal communication and you confront a difficult task. Facial expression also flows so rapidly because of its spontaneous nature that you will miss some facial expression because of its sheer quickness, and you will miss other facial expression because of limited eye contact. With an understanding of these problems, however, you can work to use facial expression more effectively in your small-group discussions.

Eye (gaze)

Communication with the eyes is also referred to as gaze communication. For ages man has described the communicative ability of the eye. Hopper (1975) records such examples as Chaucer's, "Paradise stood formed in her eye," and Ben Jonson's "Drink to me only with thine eyes and I will pledge with mine."

As a part of the face, eyes are sometimes considered a part of facial communication. There are several important characteristics of the eye that you should observe for their strong communicative features. Eyes are basically receivers of information and we usually have eye contact because we want to receive the nonverbal communication of others. In this sense, eyes serve as our "ear-equivalent" in nonverbal communication, and they tell others in our group that we are "listening." In American culture, strong eye contact has been found to be very important in establishing status and power. Birdwhistle (1970) has developed elaborate classification of eyelid movement and other aspects of the eye in his research and has found the eye area a very important source of nonverbal signals. A good discussion participant with a keen interest in the participation of all the others in the group will maintain active eye contact.

Gestures

In the last century, scholars interested in oratory and public speaking developed whole books of descriptive gestures with a feeling of certainty that specific gestures always carried certain meanings. These specific gesture classification systems were then taught in a prescriptive way in elocution classes. Today, researchers are at work classifying gestures and full body movement but we are not inclined to give specific constant meaning to each gesture. Some gestures do tend to have generally consistent meanings; holding up an index finger, for example, often represents one, first, or some similar order. But the same gesture can also connote many different meanings, and without observing the gesture in context, it is difficult to determine its true significance.

All of us use some hand gestures; indeed, some of us would be hard pressed to communicate if our hands were tied. The pointed finger, the open hand, the clenched fist, the clasped hand, and many other gestures help to convey our message. Although we cannot rigidly assign meaning to these gestures, they do tend to fall into patterns of expression such as openness or defensiveness, confidence-and self control or nervousness, and so on. We can emphasize a point, show a visual numerical signpost, display determination, reflect satisfaction, and display a host of other emotions, feelings, or emphases with hand gestures.

Body movements are as revealing as hand gestures. A shrug of the shoulders, the loosening of a tie or vest or coat, tightly crossed arms, hands clasped behind the head, legs open, legs tightly crossed, and numerous other body gestures convey meanings of their own. Again, although any one of these gestures may not have a specific constant meaning, they often communicate in the context some general meaning such as disinterest, openness, a closed mind, antagonism, or a host of other feelings.

As a discussion participant, you should be sensitive to your own body movements and those of others. For example, if Susie is rapping her fingers on the desk with a bored facial expression, you could contribute to the group by encouraging her participation. An awareness of gestural communication can help you improve your oral contributions.

Posture

There are also posture or total body movements that can convey our feelings. A slouched position, a torso on the edge of the seat, a very erect back, and many other positions can communicate our inner feelings to others. We may detect disinterest, rigidity, receptivity, a feeling of high status or power, and many other moods from observing various body postures.

Body Contact

In American culture, we use the touch of handshake as a way to express greetings. In other cultures, people use a hug or kiss or other method, while still other cultures resist body contact in similar settings. Such contact can be a way of communicating. Argyle (1975) states that touching seems to possess a primitive significance of heightened intimacy, and tends to arouse emotions. A baby hugs its parents. A lover caresses the love partner. A person in trouble is embraced by a friend. A hard-working employee gets a pat on the back from the employer. These examples reflect the numerous ways we use body contact to communicate.

Although you may not have a lot of opportunity for body contact in your small-group discussion, or you may resist body contact because of your preference, you should be aware of nonverbal communication signals as powerful communicators in certain contexts. In the small group, a gentle touch on the arm of the person next to you with an oral or other nonverbal communication signal can be a successful way to build group relationship.

Proxemic

The word "proxemic" comes from "proxemity" and relates to space and territory. Small-group communication in the discussion format has a reasonably fixed spatial arrangement by its very nature. A "small" group can only spread out so far and, of course, usually operates close together around a table or a group of chairs that keeps all group members "socially" close. In Chapter 2 we discussed the physical arrangements; here we are discussing how distance and space can communicate.

Have you ever been in a theater and have a large person sit next to you, overtaking your armrest? Have you ever been in a sports arena with stripes marked on a flat bench to designate seating area and have your space invaded by those on either side who kept inching down? Have you ever been frustrated in an auditorium by people constantly walking through an aisle in front of you and disrupting your view of a stage or screen? These are all examples of territorial invasion. In order for there to be such an invasion, however, there must be some basis for a feeling of possession of territory. We all establish territorial boundaries around ourselves. They may change in size and shape, grow larger or smaller, more rigid or more flexible, but each of us maintains some boundary of personal territory.

The most frequent violation of territory occurs by physical displacement, but we can also violate the territory of others in other ways. If a discussion participant monopolizes the oral mode, other participants may feel a violation of their protected territory, a right to have some portion of time in the oral mode. Perhaps as a discussion participant you have done some good research and you come to the discussion well prepared with documentation. If another participant just picked up some of your written research, without asking, and began reading it, you would likely have anxiety of some level because your personal territory (your possession of research material) has been invaded. Eyes can penetrate your space just as excessive noise can interfere with your interest in lower volume.

Our discussion of body contact as a form of kinesic communication dealt with an aspect of spatial separation among individuals. Overcoming physical distance can help to overcome differences stemming from persuasions or feelings. Group members in discussion are therefore encouraged to position themselves close together and to engage in other physical contacts outside of the discussion session, such as eating lunch together, walking to the library together, and so on. This is the principle that operates in the fraternity and sorority systems. Frequent contact increases a feeling of belonging and can help enhance group spirit.

Artifactual

The term "artifactual communication" is derived from the word "artifacts," the decorative trappings that surround us physically. You have actively been associated with physical appearance as a form of nonverbal communication although you may not have considered it a form of communication. Most young people are highly sensitive to the appropriate dress and grooming styles of their generation. If long hair is in vogue, they tend to wear their hair long. If dress hem styles are long, their dresses go long. If "everyone" wears blue jeans, then they wear blue jeans. We participate in this form of nonverbal communication because it says something about us: We are in style, we know what is in vogue.

We have patterns of dress, for example, in our society that serve more or less to stereotype us. In a general way, certain patterns of dress communicate status, position, power, authority, or other distinctions. A dark business suit is the dress of a highly successful business or professional man; a uniform, hat, and badge are the trademarks of a police or security officer; a white dress and cap are the sign of a nurse or health professional. Beyond these indications of "uniforms" as communicators, there are those who believe that dress communicates much more. John Malloy's fascinating book discusses in laymen's terms how to *Dress for Success*. The author reports findings as to possible meanings behind certain colors, fabrics, styles, and other aspects of dress. As a participant in discussion, we should be concerned with our own physical appearance. Neatness, cleanliness, and good grooming in general can help you have a more positive influence in a group.

Vocalization

Vocalized communication is also called paralanguage and refers to vocal features other than the actual formation of the audible word symbol. We often mention a speaker's "tone of voice" when describing if the person sounded angry, disturbed, delighted, sad, or in some other emotional state. This reference to tone of voice is a recognition that our voice pitch, intensity, projection, or other factors carry a meaning somewhat separate from the actual words communicated. For example, the tone of voice would be quite different for these two exchanges: first, "Here doggie, here pup!" and, second, "You dog! You dirty dog!" In the first instance a feeling of pleasure is communicated with the voice as the words are spoken. In the second case, a feeling of disgust and disdain should accompany the words.

In the small-group setting, participants do not have the full range of flexibility with paralanguage as there is opportunity for in a large public speaking situation. The small-group setting calls for a certain range of vocal cues appropriate to an intimate setting. Nevertheless, there is a range of vocal inflection available for use that can help you communicate more feeling than is possible with words, and at the same time you should be sensitive to listening for and interpreting the paralanguage vocal cues that other participants in the small group will use.

There are other types of nonverbal communication such as time, taste, and smell but these have little relevance, if any, for small-group communication.

Observing and Interpreting Nonverbal Communication

As we have discussed each of the nonvebal communication systems, we have stressed the need for being sensitive to other members in your group who may be communicating at different times through the different systems. This sensitivity to and alertness to observation is critical, for, as we mentioned earlier, your eyes are your "ears" for nonverbal communication.

The mere observation of nonverbal communication phenomena will not result in any significant gain in communication for you without some interpretation. We have already warned you against assigning specific meaning to nonverbal communi-

Nonverbal Dimensions of Group Communication

cation signals without considering contextual and cultural aspects. A given nonverbal communication signal may occur in isolation, but more likely a signal occurs as a part of a concert, a stream of nonverbal signals perhaps accompanied occasionally by verbal communication. The signals have significant interrelationships and the meaning of such signals should be considered in the context of their flow.

Since nonverbal communication can be both precise and vague, our treatment in this text for students of small groups deals with the interpretation of meaning of nonverbal communication in general categories. Clearly there are many others. These descriptions of categories of meaning are general and are intended only to give you some limited ideas for "reading" nonverbal communication. Later in this chapter a series of pictures will give you some specific illustrations for you to use to try your skill in interpreting nonverbal communication.

Open/Closed

The open/closed category indicates a person's willingness or lack of willingness to share openly with other members of the group in the discussion. The individual who is open will express nonverbally the desire to listen to others and to give serious consideration to the points of view expressed by all members of the group. The individual who presents nonverbally a closed attitude will exhibit nonverbal behavior indicating disinterest or an unwillingness to hear the other members of the group.

The following are several examples of nonverbal communication that may in certain contexts exhibit this category of meaning. Arms relaxed on the table or the lap may demonstrate openness while arms folded tightly across the chest may reflect a closed attitude. In similar manner, uncrossed legs may indicate openness whereas tightly crossed legs may reflect a closed feeling.

Confident/Uncertain

Nonverbally a person also gives off a communicative feeling that can be classified by the other members of the group as an air of confidence or a feeling of uncertainty. The confident group member will exhibit behavior nonverbally that demonstrates that the individual is in control of the situation as desired and the participant is comfortable with the group. On the other hand, the uncertain individual will give off nonverbal signs of being uncomfortable in the group and unsure of the individual's role as a participant in the group discussion.

Here are some possible examples that may in certain contexts demonstrate this type of meaning. Arms raised with hands clasped behind the head may represent the posture of a confident participant. An insecure person may keep arms and hands between himself and other group members. A secure group member may show a calm demeanor and pleasant facial expression. An uncertain participant may have a worried, tense facial expression in the eyes or forehead or may exhibit a number of nervous gestures such as drumming fingers on the table, biting fingernails, wringing hands, gripping pencil or book tightly, or some other similar gesture.

Pensive/Aggressive

The aggressive person may give off signs that reflect an action orientation, a desire to accomplish tasks. In contrast, the pensive person may demonstrate nonverbally a desire to be more thoughtful, to work at a slower pace, and to be more methodical and in less of a rush to perform specific tasks or to accomplish the goal.

Here are some examples of nonverbal communication behavior that might, in certain contexts, demonstrate this. A pensive group discussion participant may show a thoughtful nature by leaning back in a chair. The aggressive participant, in contrast, might sit on the edge of the chair, ready for every opportunity to contribute to the discussion. The thoughtful participant might have one arm across the chest with one arm and hand to the face, perhaps the hand stroking the chin. This might be a pensive pose, but the aggressive participant might seize an opportunity to push a hand gesture into the middle of the group to show an aggressive desire for involvement.

In explaining some broad categories of possible interpretation,

Nonverbal Dimensions of Group Communication 121

we have given some specific types of nonverbal behavior as examples. The nonverbal behavior mentioned as examples would not occur in isolation, of course, but rather in concert with other nonverbal communication and the verbal communication flow as well. In some cases, however, a participant may be commenting orally and displaying one type of feeling, while at the same time communicating a different feeling nonverbally. This would create dissonance in the other group members. A discussion participant should be skilled in reading nonverbal communication of the two modes. A discussion participant unskilled in nonverbal communication may be fooled into believing only the oral communication.

Test Your Nonverbal Reading Ability

In this chapter we have discussed nonverbal communication systems. We have given some attention to how you can interpret nonverbal communication as well as to how you can use nonverbal communication. Now you have a chance to test your reading ability of nonverbal communication. We have adapted a plan from Gulley and Leathers (1977) using photographs of students to give you an opportunity for some experience in interpreting nonverbal communication. Examine each photograph in the following pages and consider carefully the nonverbal communication displayed by each participant in view. Understanding that you have a very limited knowledge of the context, try nevertheless to write out in general statements what meaning you perceive is being communicated nonverbally by each participant. Once you have completed your attempt at interpretation of the nonverbal communication in each photograph, compare your description with the text's description for each photo. The text's descriptions are printed at the end of this chapter.

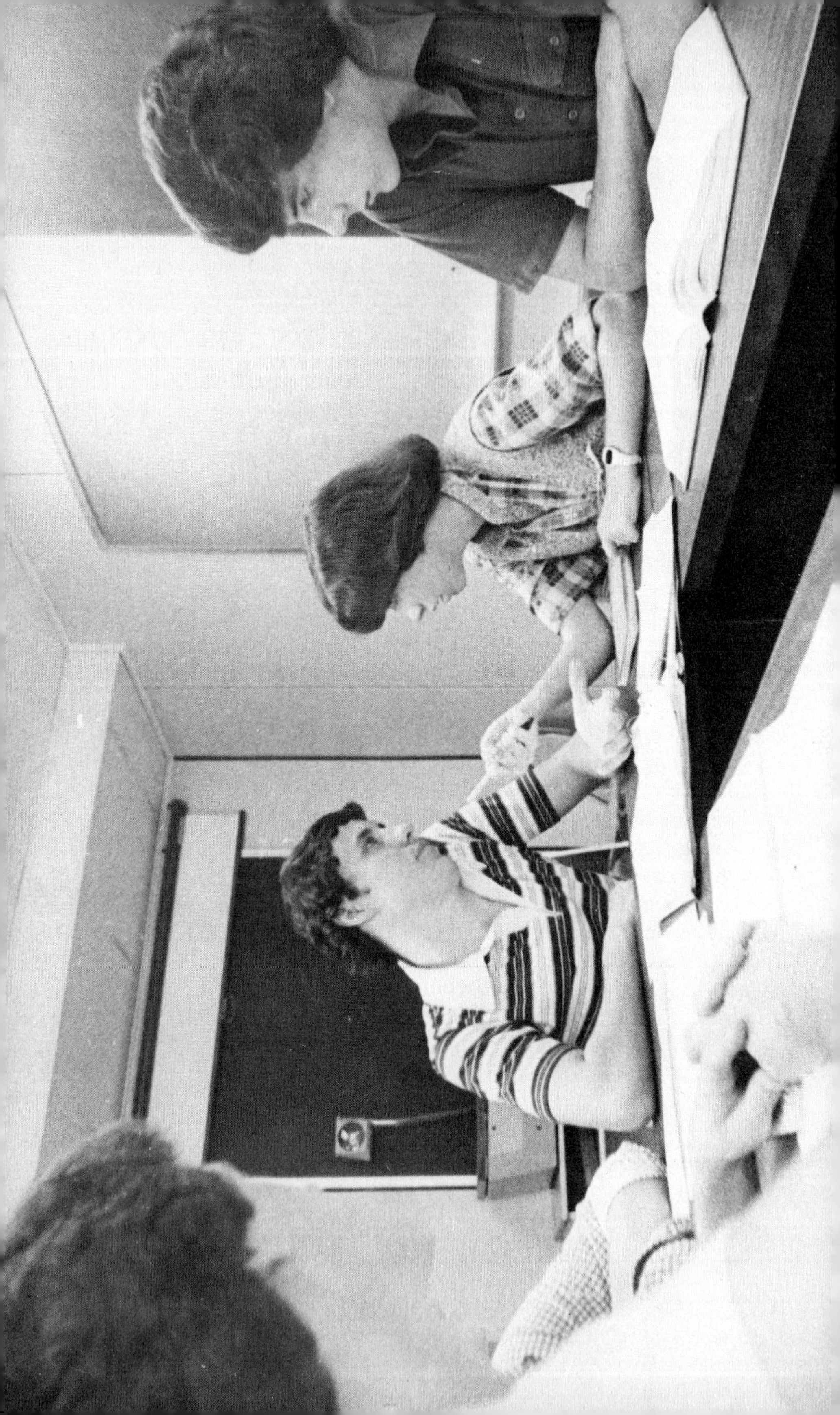

Photograph #1

Using the nonverbal communication systems and broad categories of meaning described in this chapter, write a brief description of your interpretation or "reading" of the non verbal communication exhibited by each person in the photograph.

Comments:

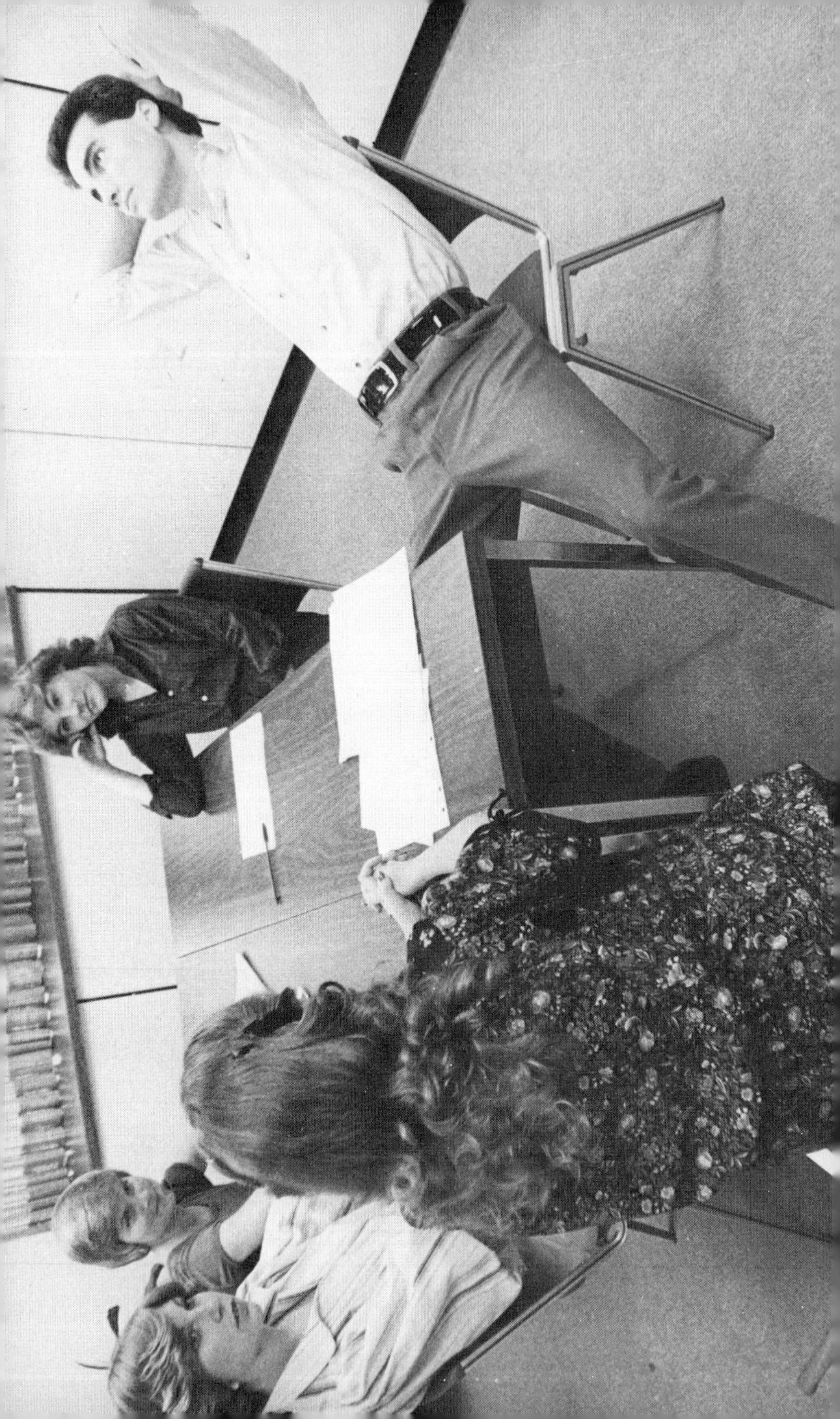

Photograph #2

Using the nonverbal communication systems and broad categories of meaning described in this chapter, write a brief description of your interpretation or "reading" of the nonverbal communication exhibited by each person in the paragraph.

Comments:

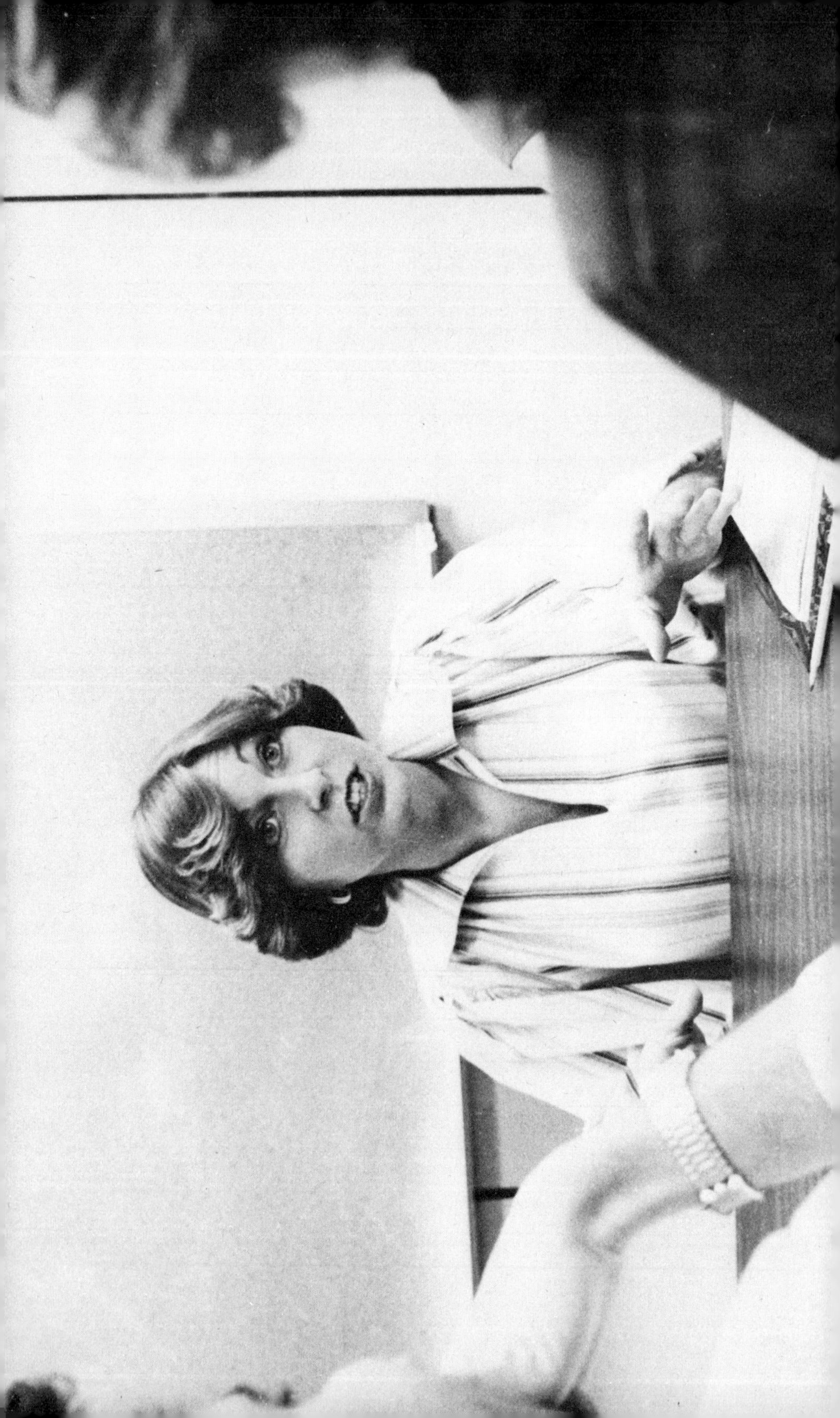

Photograph #3

Using the nonverbal communication systems and broad categories of meaning described in this chapter, write a brief description of your interpretation or "reading" of the nonverbal communication exhibited by each person in the photograph.

Comments:

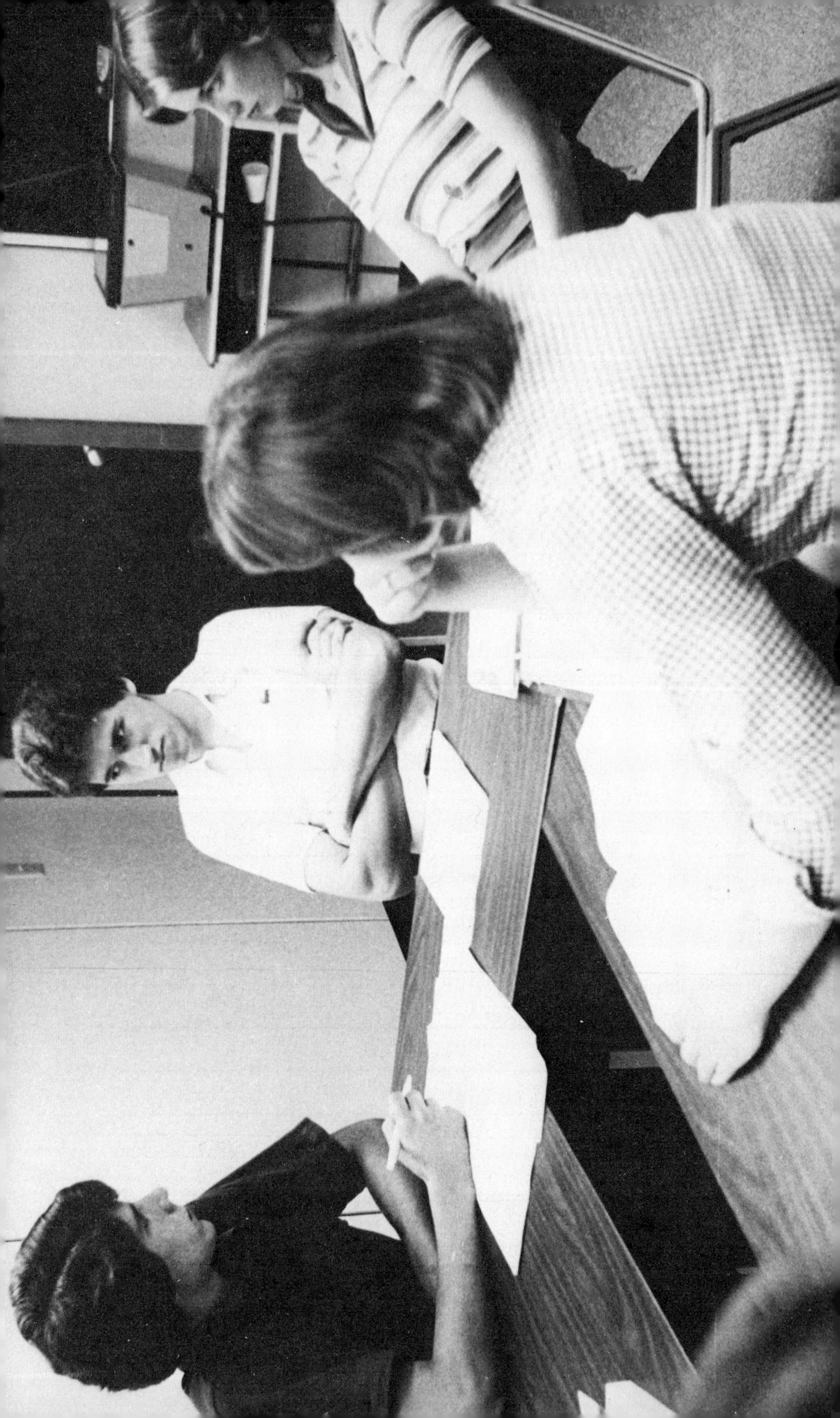

Photograph #4

Using the nonverbal communication systems and broad categories of meaning described in this chapter, write a brief description of your interpretation or "reading" of the nonverbal communication exhibited by each person in the photograph.

Comments:

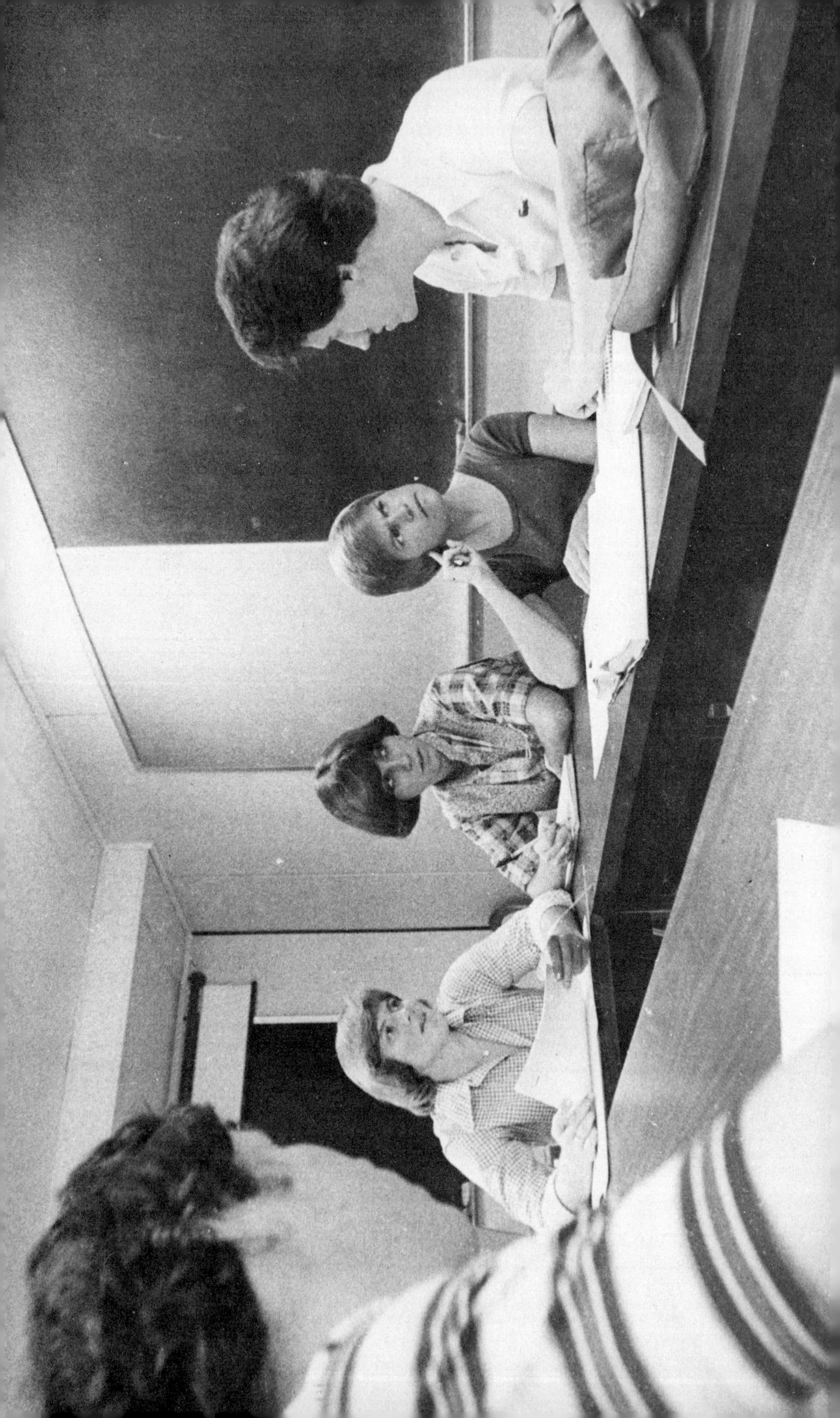

Photograph #5

Using the nonverbal communication systems and broad categories of meaning described in this chapter, write a brief description of your interpretation or "reading" of the nonverbal communication exhibited by each person in the photograph.

Comments:

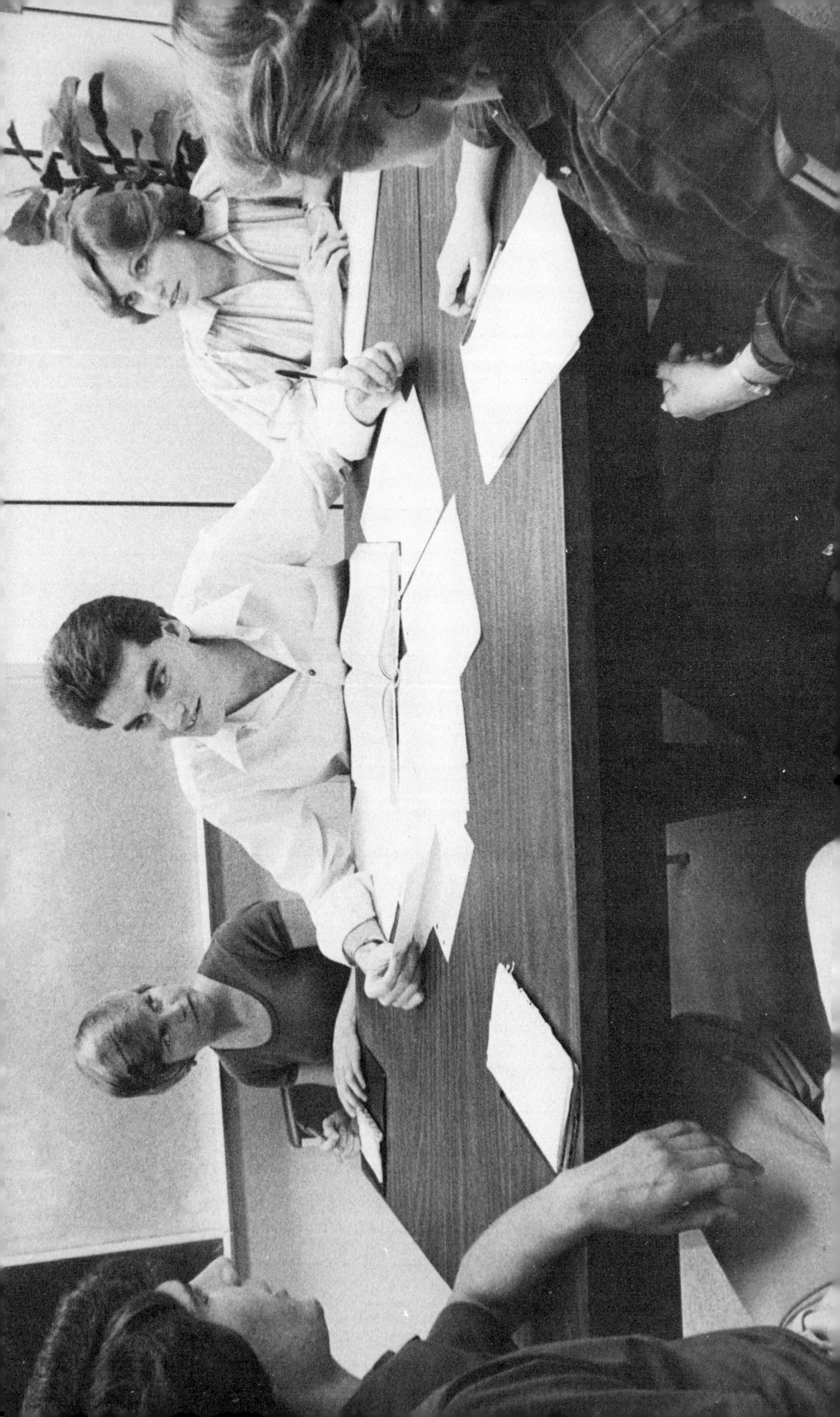

Photograph #6

Using the nonverbal communication systems and broad categories of meaning described in this chapter, write a brief description of your interpretation or "reading" of the nonverbal communication exhibited by each person in the paragraph.

Comments:

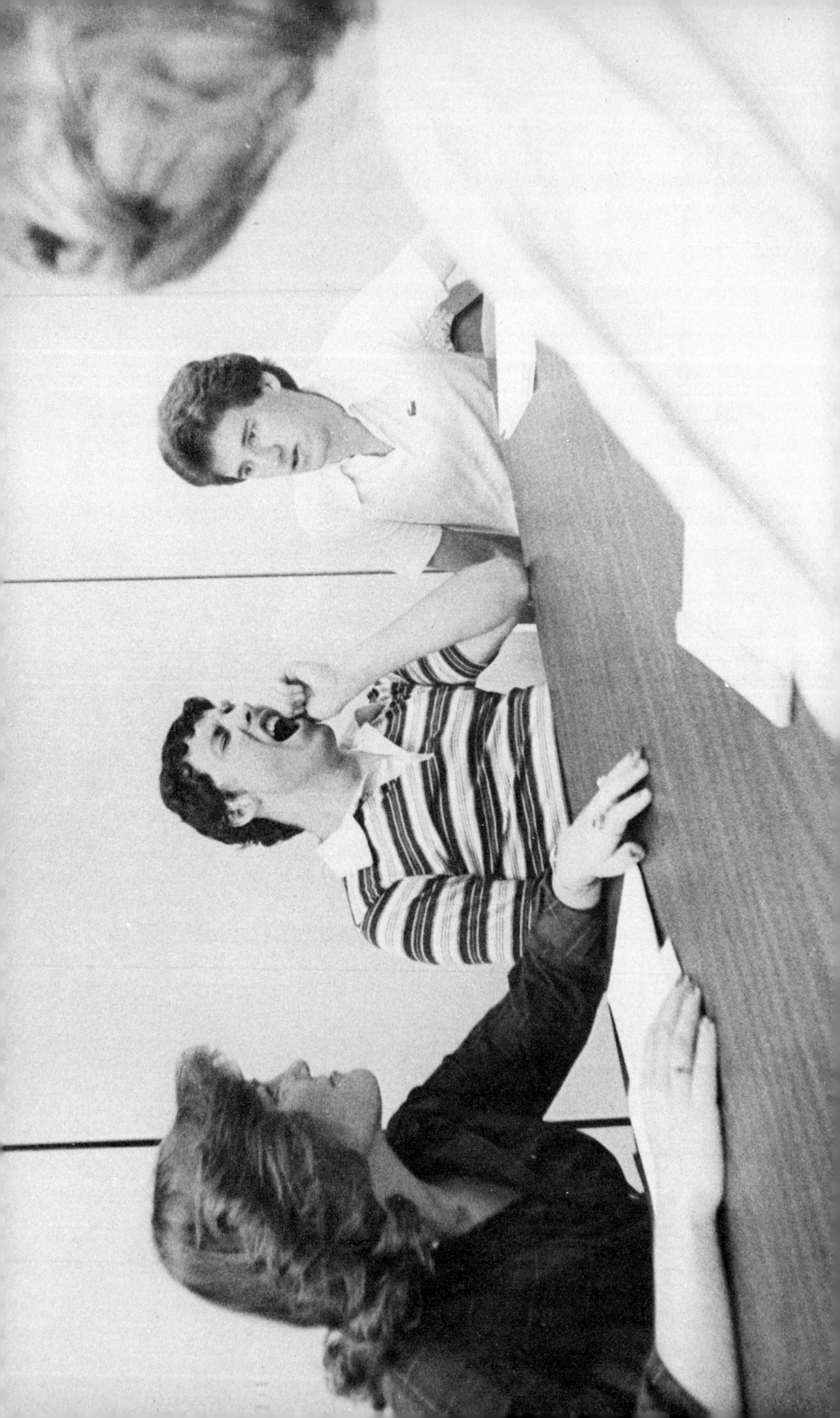

Photograph #7

Using the nonverbal communication systems and broad categories of meaning described in this chapter, write a brief description of your interpretation or "reading" of the nonverbal communication exhibited by each person in the photograph.

Comments:

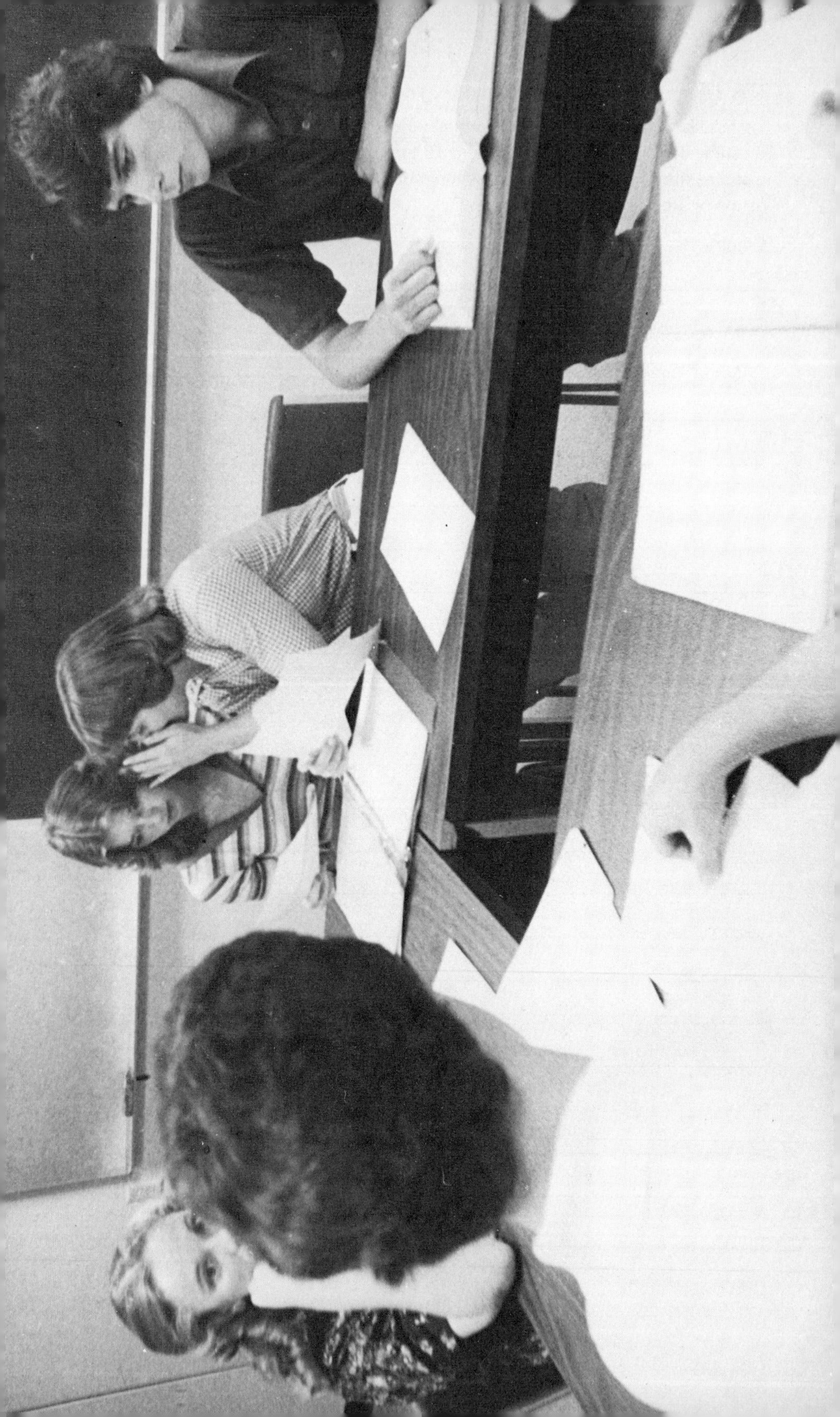

Photograph #8

Using the nonverbal communication systems and broad categories of meaning described in this chapter, write a brief description of your interpretation or "reading" of the nonverbal communication exhibited by each person in the photograph.

Comments:

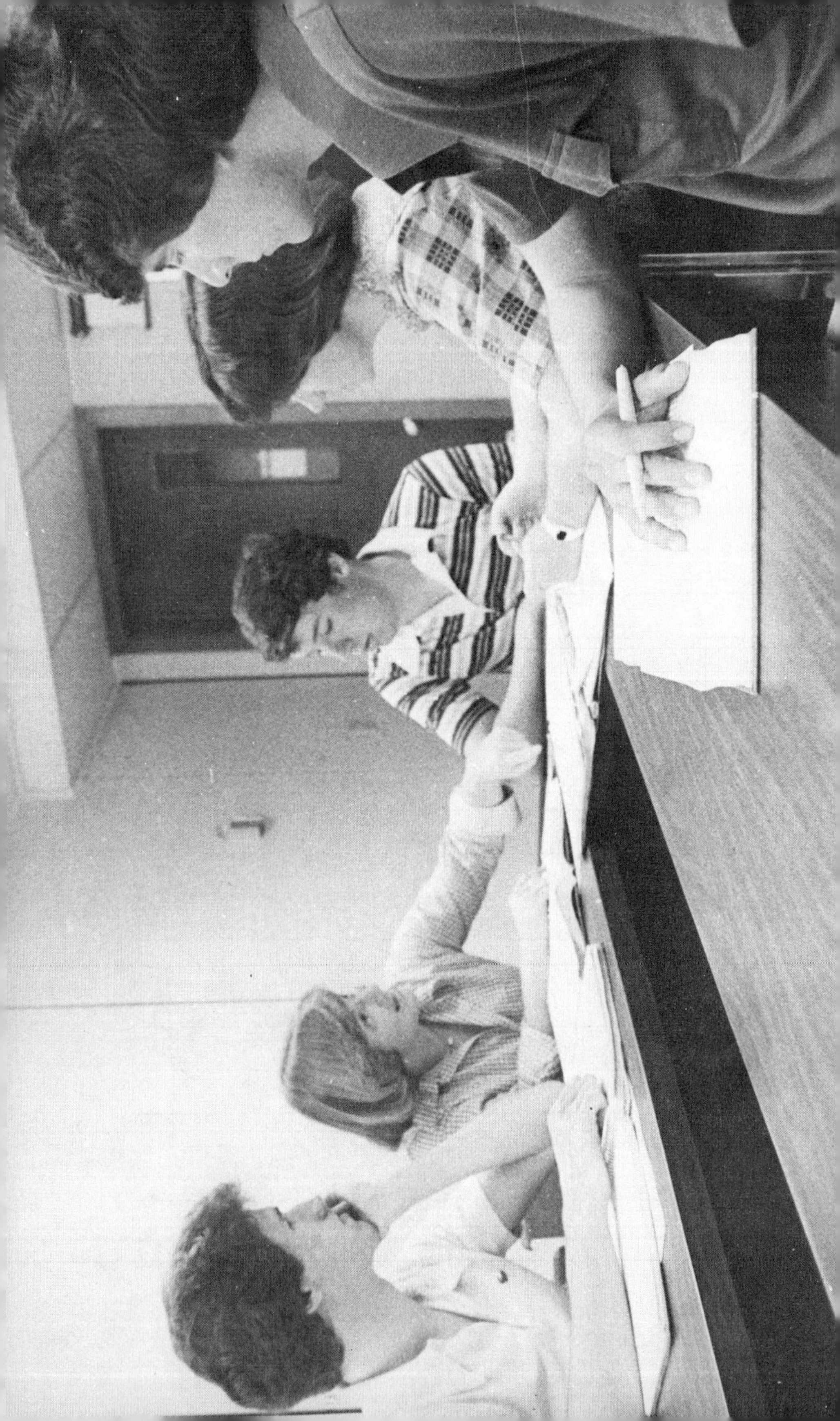

Photograph #9

Using the nonverbal communication systems and broad categories of meaning described in this chapter, write a brief description of your interpretation or "reading" of the nonverbal communication exhibited by each person in the photograph.

Comments:

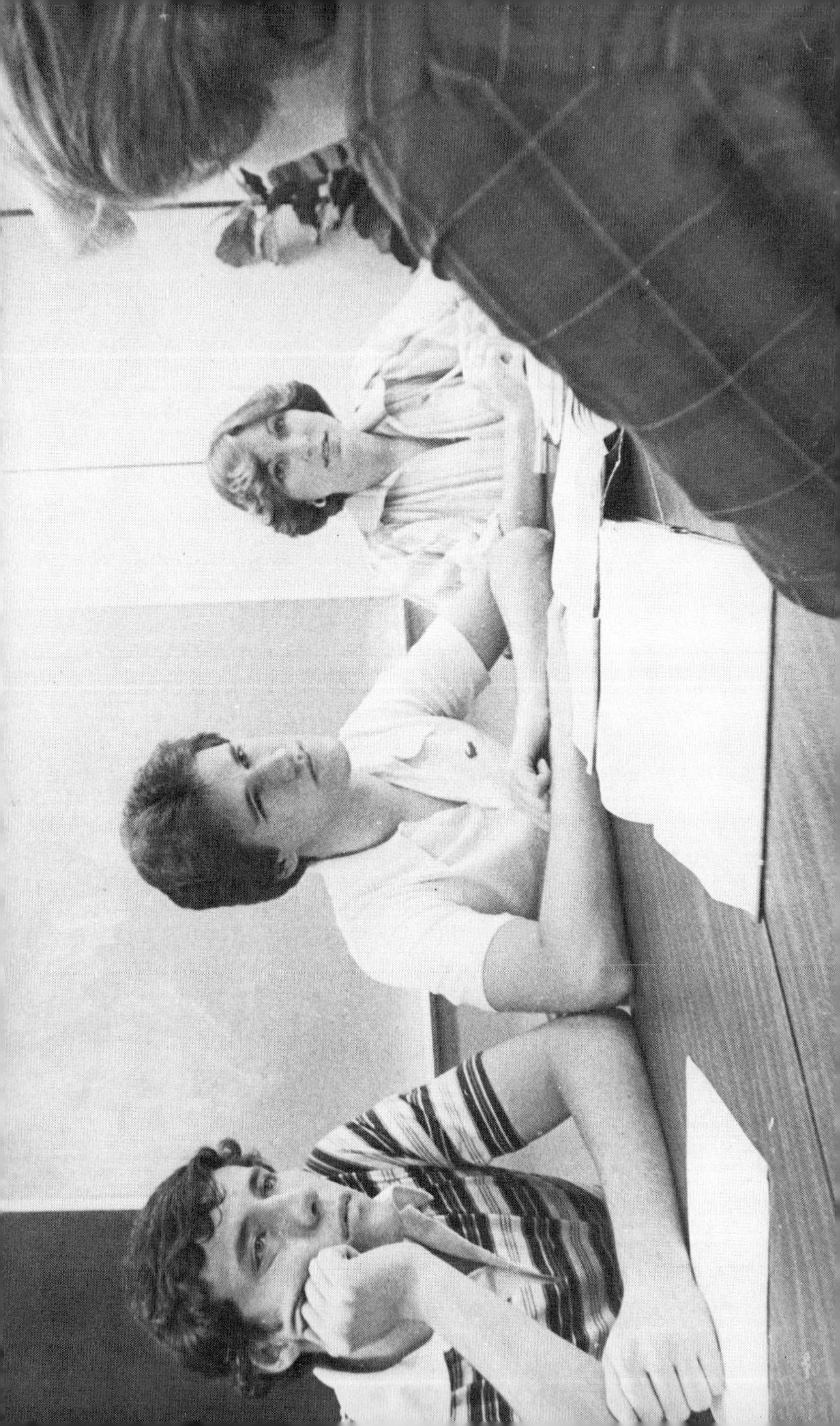

Photograph #10

Using the nonverbal communication systems and broad categories of meaning described in this chapter, write a brief description of your interpretation or "reading" of the nonverbal communication exhibited by each person in the photograph.

Comments:

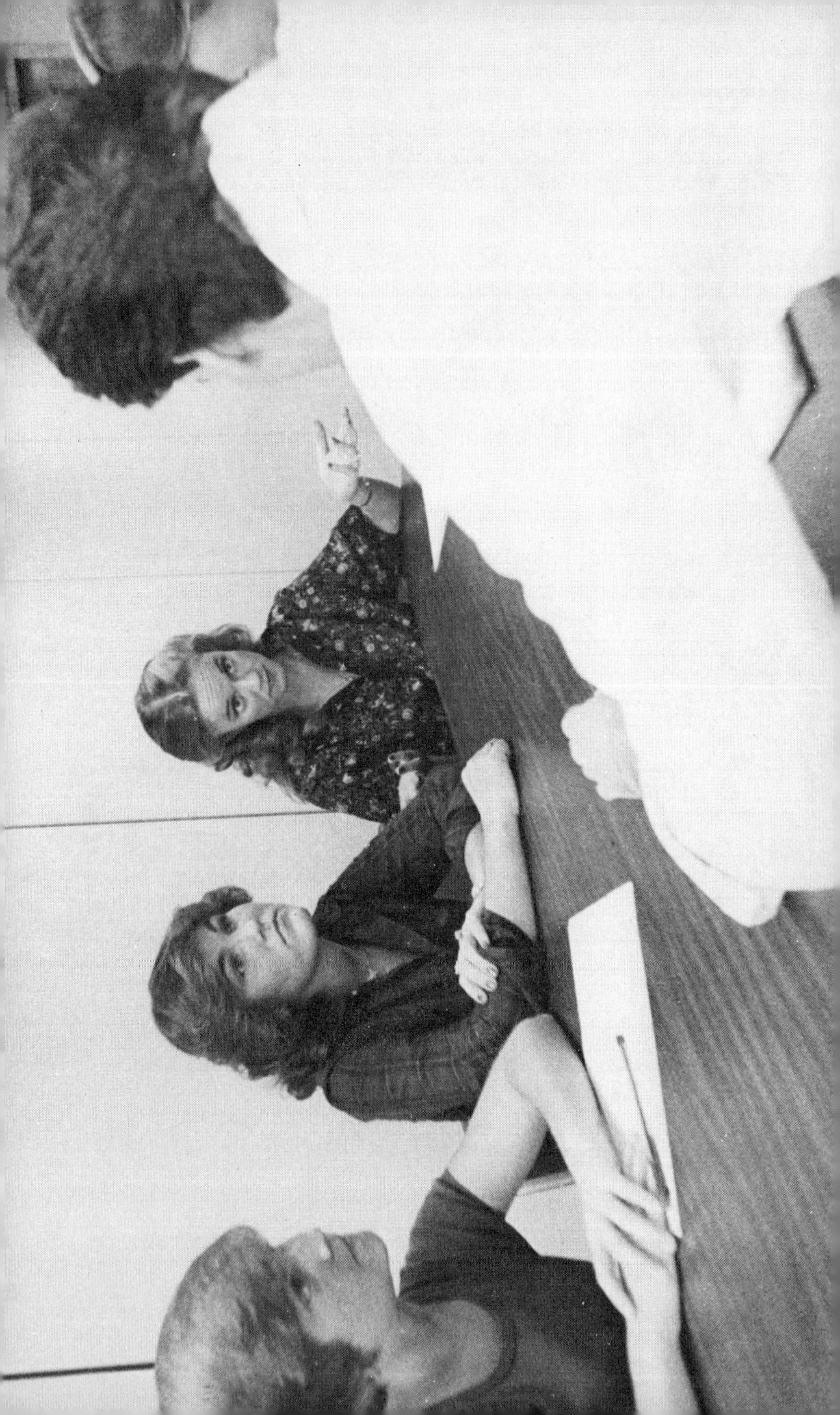

Photograph #11

Using the nonverbal communication systems and broad categories of meaning described in this chapter, write a brief description of your interpretation or "reading" of the nonverbal communication exhibited by each person in the photograph.

Comments:

143

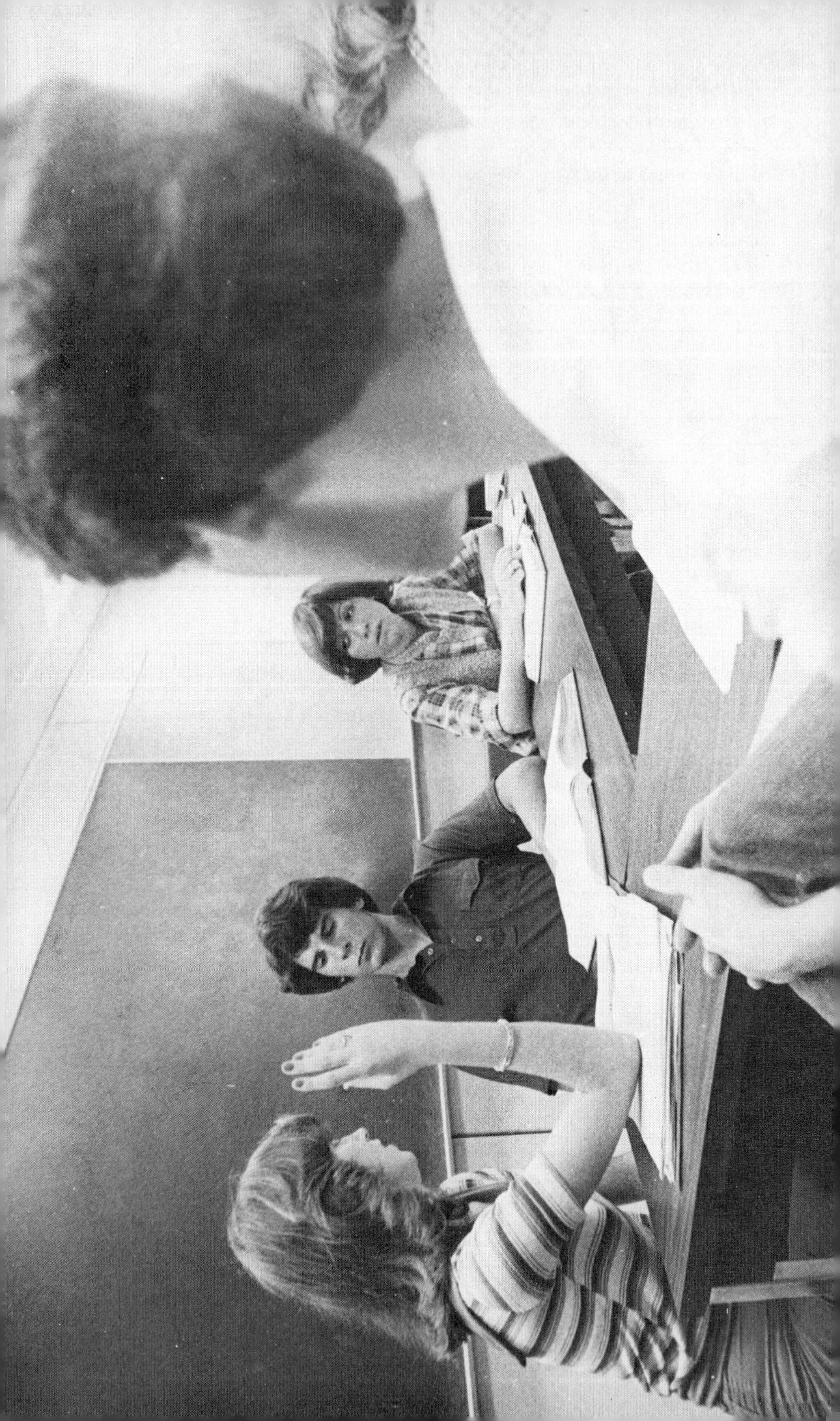

Photograph #12

Using the nonverbal communication systems and broad categories of meaning described in this chapter, write a brief description of your interpretation or "reading" of the nonverbal communication exhibited by each person in the photograph.

Comments:

Summary

This chapter defined nonverbal communication as all communication except that which is coded in words. We discussed the evidence and use of nonverbal communication in society and the particular relevance of nonverbal communication to small-group communication and discussion.

Nonverbal communication was viewed as a complex with a series of systems, including kinesic communication, proxemic communication, artifactual communication, and vocal communication. Readers were cautioned against oversimplification of nonverbal communication, and it was stressed that nonverbal communication should be viewed in context and with cultural considerations. We explored also the interrelationship of the nonverbal to the verbal.

Some explanation of observation and interpretation was offered, and series of photographs of particular small group settings was provided to give readers a chance to experiment with interpreting nonverbal communication. An explanation of these photographs follows.

Explanation of Photographs

Photograph #1

There are five people participating in this small-group discussion, but at the time of this picture two discussants are involved in a personal exchange. Other members of the discussion seem to remain involved, however, as their posture, eye contact, and facial expression indicate interest in the exchange occurring between the two members.

In the two-person exchange, the discussant on the right appears to be taking an aggressive position with her body leaning forward over the table and with a clenched hand directed toward the other member. The discussant on the left seems to be responding with body language that says, "So what?" Notice that his shoulder is raised in a "shrug" position, his hand is open, and his arm extended; notice also the tilt of his head and his facial expression—all of which might point to his rejection of the other discussant by the appearance of a closed mind.

Photograph #2

There are five participants in this discussion. The participant seen from the back appears to be speaking at this time. Notice that she is positioned sitting on the front edge of the seat. Three of the other participants appear to be involved in the discussion with eye contact directed toward the member speaking. These three members exhibit various pleasant facial expressions but all appear to be involved in listening. One member, however, is apparently daydreaming, leaning back in his chair and with his eyes indicating a distant gaze. The participant speaking has her hands clasped in a closed position while the apparently daydreaming participant is in a totally open position with legs spread and arms open with his hands behind his head.

Photograph #3

Although there are several participants in this discussion, the photograph focuses on the participant speaking. The eyes of this participant are extremely talkative, showing an intense desire to communicate and be understood, and the eyes exude a look of confidence. The raised eyebrows and wrinkled forehead express intensity and the desire for acceptance. The participant seems to be leaning toward the table with hand gestures extending in an explaining position, both characteristics also reinforcing an intense desire to communicate, to be understood, and to have a point accepted.

Photograph #4

There are three discussants in clear view in this picture with one discussant's back in view. All participants appear to be looking to the discussant on the left who is speaking. This discussant is leaning on his elbows on the table with a pen gripped in his hand. He exhibits an overall appearance of tightness and possible nervousness. The next participant to the right is sitting back in his seat, away from the discussant talking, and has his hands in a locked fold across his chest. By his proxemic and gestural communication he appears removed and uninvolved, perhaps uninterested or perhaps opposed to the other participant. This participant's facial expression seems to say, "I'm not sure I like you or like what you're saying!" The third member of the group, the one in the picture, is leaning far back in her chair expressing a sense of distance, a sense of aloofness from the discussion and from the other members.

Photograph #5

There are five participants in view in this picture. The participant on the far right appears to be speaking and the other members of the group are demonstrating various levels of interest. The participant second from the left seems to be attempting to inject a comment into the discussion, showing an open and moderately aggressive posture. The group member third from the left appears alert, attentive, and interested—positive body language. The group member second from the right demonstrates a frown in the forehead area and conveys a puzzled expression that tends to convey a negative reaction to the other group members. All other members in the group seem to be presenting generally positive body language.

Photograph #6

There are five participants in view in this photograph. The participant in the center has staked out considerable territory in table space in which his notes have "taken over" the table. In addition, he is leaning up over the table with his arms outstretched around his material presenting the impression to other participants that he is guarding the personal territory that he has staked out. Notice that the participants seated next to this member appear to be pushed to the side and overtaken by the possessive group participant. This seizure of an excessively large amount of space invades the territory of other participants and creates a negative, nonverbal impact on other members of the group.

Nonverbal Dimensions of Group Communication 149

Photograph #7

There are three discussants principally in view in this photograph. The participant in the middle, by yawning, nonverbally is displaying a lack of interest in the discussion that is taking place. Also, notice that this individual member has no material on the table in front of him and he may be suffering from a lack of preparation for the discussion. This lack of preparation could be the source of his apparent boredom since such a person would not be prepared to actively participate. An overt act of boredom, such as an open yawn, may have a very negative impact on other members of the group.

Photograph #8

There are five participants in view in this photograph. The discussant with his back in view appears to be orally participating at this time. Two other members of the group seem to be directing their attention toward this participant. The other two members of the group are engaged in a private conversation, which is sometimes referred to as "mini-discussion" since it is a two-person discussion within a larger group. This behavior can be antagonizing to other members of the group who may wish to know the information being discussed by the small subgroup. Other group members may become irritated by this type of behavior and may tend to isolate discussants who engage in "mini-discussions."

Photograph #9

There are five participants in view in this photograph. Looking left to right, the participant on the far left is in a pensive posture, listening to and observing the discussion that appears to be going on between the two participants. The next participant is emphatically making a point with a pointed finger and an extended arm. Notice the apparent intensity also emphasized by the facial expression, raised eyes and tilted head. The third participant is indicating an apparent interest in the vigorous, physical gesturing; he may feel caught in a cross-fire in what appears to be a tense exchange between two of the group members. The fourth participant is also exhibiting an intense feeling with clenched fists, extended arms reaching toward the participant across the table, and gritted teeth. The fifth participant is observing the exchange but demonstrates no apparent threat since he is removed from the cross-fire. Intense, sometimes bitter exchanges of this type hamper group cohesiveness and may raise the anxiety levels of all participants.

Photograph #10

There are four participants in this photograph with one of the participants' back in view. The participant to the far left is demonstrating an interested attitude. The eyes indicate a careful listening to the other participant and an interest in the discussion. The fixture of the arms—the fact that one arm is folded and one arm is to the cheek area—represents a pensive gesture. The next participant exhibits a partially closed nonverbal sign with his arms folded loosely in front of him and resting on the table. The facial expression of this participant is one of interest, but it also indicates a quizzical concern. This participant appears to be having trouble understanding a point or perhaps may be in disagreement with the point made. The third participant appears to be having trouble understanding a point or perhaps may be in disagreement with the point made. The third participant appears more open and receptive while at the same time expressing interest through the eye contact and facial expression.

Photograph #11

There are three main participants in view with another participant's back in view in this photograph. There seems to be an exchange occurring in the group between the female participant third from left and the male participant whose back is in view. In this two-way exchange the female participant is making a combined hand gesture and strong facial expression. The wrinkled forehead may indicate one of several possible meanings, such as "That's just the way I see it" or "Do you understand?" The open hand gesture with the arms slightly extended probably represents another nonverbal communication signal that reinforces the facial expression.

This type of body language carries some negative impact and may cause the other participants to feel that there is little opportunity for reply without antagonizing this participant. A person may make a "loaded" statement, or may ask a rhetorical or "loaded" question while using this gesture or facial expression to emphasize the "obvious" answer. The other two female participants in view, their loosely folded arms and hands resting on the table, appear removed or uninvolved. The male participant with the back in view is leaning forward over the table and may be expressing intensity of interest in the discussion exchange.

Photograph #12

There are three participants clearly in view in this photograph with the back of an additional participant in view. Going from left to right, the individual to the left is making a point in the discussion. This participant is seated on the edge of her chair and is leaning forward over the table while gesturing with her hand. She is expressing keen interest and some aggressiveness with a strong desire to be heard, understood, and accepted by the other group members. The participant second from the left, with one elbow resting on the table and seated back away from the table, is communicating through proxemics some distance and also appears to have a pensive posture.

The third individual is leaning on the table and in the direction of the other participant speaking at this point in the discussion. This third participant appears to be actively interested in being involved in the discussion exchange, perhaps ready to contribute orally at the next chance. The male student with his back in view in this picture is seated back away from the table with the legs crossed and his hands clasped around his knees, reflecting a body language of a relaxed position, thoughtful and nonaggressive.

References and Further Reading

ARGYLE, MICHAEL, *Bodily Communication*. New York: International Universities Press, 1975.

BIRDWHISTLE, RAY L., *Kinesics and Context.* Philadelphia: University of Pennsylvania, 1970.
EISENBERG, ABNE M., and RALPH R. SMITH, JR., *Nonverbal Communication.* Indianapolis: Bobbs-Merrill, 1971, Chs. 1 and 2.
EKMAN, PAUL, and WALLACE V. FRIESEN, *Unmasking the Face.* Englewood Cliffs, N.J.: Prentice-Hall, 1975.
FAST, JULIUS, *Body Language.* New York: M. Evans, 1970.
GULLEY, HALBERT E., and DALE G. LEATHERS, *Communication and Group Process.* New York: Holt, Rinehart and Winston, 1977.
HOPPER, ROBERT, *Human Message Systems.* New York: Harper and Row, 1976. p. 80.
KNAPP, MARK L., *Nonverbal Communication in Human Interaction.* New York: Holt, Rinehart and Winston, 1972, p. 119.
LEATHERS, D. G., *Nonverbal Communication.* Boston: Allyn and Bacon, 1976, pp. 4–7.
MEHRABIAN, ALBERT, *Silent Messages.* Belmont, California: Wadsworth, 1971.
MOLLOY, JOHN, *Dress for Success.* New York: Wyden, 1975.
NIERENBERG, GERARD I., and HENRY H. CALERO, *How to Read People Like a Book.* New York: Hawthorn Books, 1971.
ROSENFELD, LAWRENCE B., *Human Interaction in the Small Group Setting.* Columbus: Charles E. Merrill, 1973.
ZAIDEL, SUSAN F., and ALBERT MEHRABIAN. "The Ability to Communicate and Infer Positive and Negative Attitudes Facially and Vocally," in *Advances in Communication Research,* C. David Mortensen and Kenneth K. Sereno (Eds.). New York: Harper and Row, pp. 350–60.

Leadership–Followership: A Competency Approach

OBJECTIVES:

After reading this chapter, you should be able to:

Discuss and reach a consensus agreement on the *Leadership Characteristic Worksheet*.

Define leadership and its functions.

Identify and describe the leadership behaviors of an "emergent" leader.

Identify and describe leadership–followership expectations.

Identify and describe the relationships between leader behavior and group productivity, cohesiveness, and satisfaction.

Identify and describe the relationships between person-oriented behaviors and work-oriented behaviors in followers (group members).

Identify, select, discuss, and reach a consensus agreement on the *Leadership Characteristics Situation* simulation.

Appreciate the values inherent in affecting leadership behaviors in your group by moving away from self-centered behaviors.

FUNDAMENTALS OF GROUP COMMUNICATION[1]

GENERAL KNOWLEDGE ABOUT GROUP COMMUNICATION

1. Nature/Usefulness
2. Types/Format
3. The Process and Its Phases
4. Strengths/Weaknesses

TASK DIMENSION

1. Planning/Preparation
2. Procedures/Arrangements
3. Interpersonal/Group Communication Competencies
4. Phases of Integrated Problem Solving
5. **Leadership Responsibilities**

SOCIAL DIMENSION

1. Self/Group Characteristics
2. Self/Group Concepts
3. Interpersonal/Group Attraction
4. Social Attributes
5. Dimensions of Nonverbal Behavior
6. **Leadership Characteristics**
7. Role/Status/Power
8. Mature/Immature Group Characteristics

ASSESSMENT

1. Formative/Summative
2. Individual/Group Evaluation Technique
3. Maturing Member/Group: Strengths and Weaknesses

[1] Concepts in bold face are emphasized in this chapter.

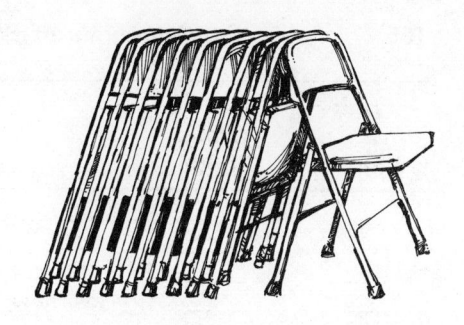

The bulk of research concerning "leadership"—its attributes and the kinds of communication behaviors associated with leaders—is abundant with points of view, but no central agreement exists on a list of characteristics intrinsic to the idea of "leadership." Before you read the following chapters, we want you to select those characteristics that you sense as more and less important for a leader to have in order to conduct a group discussion. Once you have completed the Leadership Characteristics Worksheet and your group has reached a general agreement on the same list, then you can examine what the research literature suggests about leaders and followers and the communication competencies involved in leading a discussion.

Leadership Characteristics Worksheet[1]

Name _____ Group _____

Instructions: Under the column marked "Individual Ranking," you are to rank-order the twelve characteristics listed below. Place the number (1) before the characteristic you feel is most important for a good leader, the number (2) before the second best, etc. The characteristic ranked twelfth will be least important. Later, your group is to arrive at a consensus-ranking that each of you can agree with, at least partially. This ranking is noted under the column marked "Group Ranking."

---

[1] Reproduced from The 1976 Annual Handbook for Group Facilitators, J. William Pfeiffer and John E. Jones, Editors, University Associates Publishers, Inc. (La Jolla, California, 1976), pp. 15–17.

Individual Ranking	Group Ranking	Characteristics
_____	_____	A. Maintains an orderly meeting most of the time.
_____	_____	B. Is friendly and sociable.
_____	_____	C. Has new and interesting ideas—is creative.
_____	_____	D. Listens and tries to understand others.
_____	_____	E. Is firm and decisive, not hesitant.
_____	_____	F. Admits errors openly and easily.
_____	_____	G. Makes sure everyone understands what is expected.
_____	_____	H. Provides opportunities for group members to aid in decision-making activities.
_____	_____	I. Uses praise frequently and negative criticism sparingly.
_____	_____	J. Is willing to compromise.
_____	_____	K. Follows strictly accepted rules and procedures.
_____	_____	L. Never expresses anger or dissatisfaction with others.

Leadership might best be conceived as "those acts of communication (verbal and nonverbal) that facilitate the achievement of group goals." It should be obvious that almost any aspect of group discussion from developing an agenda to the final action taken by a group may be related, to some extent, to the phenomenon of leadership. It should also be obvious that the net effects of the actual leader's efforts with a group are measurable mainly by the performance-effectiveness of the group.

Fundamentally, every situation encountered by your small group or any other similar-sized assembly of people changes the dynamics between the leader and the followers. Stogdill indicates:

> There is a scarcity of research that tests the interaction of leader personality, values, and behaviors with follower personality, values, and behaviors and the effects of such interaction upon the group. Results of several studies suggest that extreme homogeneity in leader-follower characteristics may be dysfunctional to the exercise of leadership and group performance.

Leadership–Followership: A Competency Approach

Leadership, then, is a set of functions created by a group from one or more of its members in response to their (the group's) own needs. Just being "nice" to group members and/or being stern and heavy-handed will not insure success or undermine a group's efforts to complete their work.

Although no particular style of leadership is guaranteed to be effective in *all* tasks, value, or fact/conjecture situations, we can provide some direction as to the communication factors of leaders in these three situations. For example, research in leadership behaviors indicates that the member who talks and participates the most will likely "emerge" as the group's leader. The "emergent" leader tends to differ from nonleader peers in initiating and maintaining interactions with the members of the group. The group member who tries to "emerge" as a leader tends to make such interpersonal attempts when he or she feels that his or her status is high in the group, when the member believes that he or she can actually do the necessary work, and the group perceives him to be competent to complete the task facing them. Additionally, the group member who possesses information valuable to the group's task and might therefore contribute more than other members to the solution of the group task tends to "emerge" as a leader. Finally, an emergent leader tends to spontaneously widen the group's freedom to discuss, to take action, to accept the views of less capable members, and to tolerate a wide span of popular and unpopular views from popular and not-so-popular members of the group.

It is because of our classroom experience that we recommend the natural development of the "emergent" group leader in your classroom situation. Groups such as yours tend to accept a member as their leader when he/she exhibits communicative behaviors that speed the development and accomplishment of its tasks. It is just as likely that groups such as yours can't really have any effective performance until a group identity and each member's expectations of each other gels into a structure wherein each member has the freedom to work with and respond to the leader.

Leadership–Followership Expectations

The behaviors of an emergent leader that most closely match the expectations of the group members usually produce a high degree of member satisfaction. Weinberg, Smotroff, and Pecka claim the communication behaviors of group emergent leadership to be:

1. *Openness:* a combination of the ability to receive information and a willingness to respond to other group members and their suggestions;
2. *Information:* an apparent knowledge base and the ability to organize that information to make it accessible for group problem solving;
3. *Persuasion:* the ability to influence others in the group, and to maintain a highly credible group role.

Weinberg et al. argue that *openness* and *persuasion* show significant correlations with their group observations of leadership emergence while *information* proved to be a less promising factor. In their investigations, Weinberg et al. couldn't discriminate between student group's availability of information and the organization and application of information. We must await more research before we will have a universally applicable operational definition of group leadership.

What we do know is that group members tend to be better satisfied working under a leader skilled in human relations (the Weinberg et al. category of *openness*) than one skilled in solving problems. Usually, groups have been found to be satisfied with a people-oriented leader when he/she is not under a great deal of stress while facing a difficult group problem. When the stressful dynamics of a group's problem and the individual needs of a group are present, the people-oriented human relations leader reverts to a characteristic style of leading and behaving with the group. Research indicates that the same general pattern occurs for the task-oriented leader when faced with a stressful group problem; in this case, he or she is high in task behavior and low in person-related behavior.

When the communication behaviors of an emergent leader most closely match the expectations of the group members, there is usually a high degree of overall member satisfaction. When discrepancies occur between what followers expect and how leaders behave there can be a negative effect on solving the group's problems. When there is such a gap in communication expectations, group members usually compensate by urging for a heavy dose of interpersonal "liking for each other," the *esprit-de-corp* of the "team," as a way to counterbalance too much or too little task structure coming from the leader.

In the final analysis, the acid test of leader behaviors and follower expectations rests solely on one common denominator, the performance of the group. The best evidence argues that a group appears to select as leader the member who creates the expectation that he/she will be able to maintain the group's efforts to reach its goal, to facilitate the achievement of the group's task, and to ensure one group's cohesiveness. That is a tall order for anyone to accomplish!

In the real sense of the word "competent," any member of a group seeking to develop as a leader needs to develop his or her behaviors to include person-related and task-related skills that focus on *productivity*. The overriding communication skills necessary for leadership are blends of "attention to the task" and "building group cohesiveness."

We need to examine now the important, connective relationship between group performance and leadership in order to understand just what does seem to work and what doesn't seem to work. After all, when all is said and done, the fundamental question remains, What communication competencies must a leader possess in order to have a solid "batting average" with the group as to their abilities to *solve* a problem and to be *satisfied* with that product?

Leadership and Group Performance

Throughout this chapter, we have leaned heavily on Stogdill's survey of leadership studies for directions, suggestions, and ultimately, for guarded prescriptions of the kinds of communication skills that need to be learned and mastered. The styles of leadership most often described in the literature, summarized in Stogdill's work, can be found in any book on group discussion, e.g., autocratic or authoritarian, democratic, and *laissez-faire* or free-reign. The research on leadership styles and what can one learn from each of these efforts as to what to do or what not to do have filled one chapter after another in numerous group discussion texts.

Instead of discussing these styles of leadership, we really want to know what lessons can be learned from research conducted on leader behavior and its relationship to group productivity, cohesiveness, and satisfaction. Again, the survey of relevant studies is summarized best by Stogdill:

1. Person-oriented patterns of leader behavior are not consistently related to productivity.
2. Among the work-oriented patterns, only those behaviors that maintain role differentiation and let followers know what to expect are consistently related to group productivity.
3. Among the person-oriented behaviors, only those providing freedom for member participation in group activities and showing concern for followers' welfare and comfort are consistently related to group cohesiveness.
4. Among the work-oriented behaviors, only the pattern that structures member expectations is uniformly related to group cohesiveness.
5. All the person-oriented behaviors tend to be related positively to follower satisfaction.
6. Among the work-oriented behaviors, only those structuring expectations are more often than not related positively to follower satisfaction.

To use that word again, "fundamentally," we are suggesting strongly that the student learn from the research on leadership that a combination of *person* and *work* behaviors are required to gain any degree of success in group performance and group satisfaction.

Up to this point, we have provided you with a general, though

Leadership–Followership: A Competency Approach 161

comprehensive, view of leadership and followership, their relationships, and a "survival skills" breakdown of a "work–play" approach to acquiring competency in leadership. So, where are we and what are the most important communication skills a leader should acquire and learn how to master from situation to situation? We would emphasize one pattern of communication behavior: providing a formal agenda–*structure* to meet the various *expectations* of group members as they face the solving of a problem. Members of numerous organizations, e.g., students, businessmen, church groups, social fraternities, and the like *depend* on their leaders to justify the group's existence and to satisfy the group's collective expectations regarding each other's place in the group (including the leader).

Leadership Characteristics— A Simulated Problem-Solving Experience

It is time now to come to grips with the research information and suggestions provided so far in this chapter in a unique and meaningful group experience. We have provided below a tested and highly useful simulation for you and your group that is a follow-up exercise to the Leadership Characteristics Worksheet at the beginning of this chapter. We suggest that your group spend as much class time as possible on the project in order to deal with the competencies required to fill each committee chairmanship.

Leadership Characteristics Situation Description Sheet [2]

You are one of six coordinators who will plan a weekend activity program for your organization. The task of the group is to select five committee chairmen for the event. Twelve persons have volunteered.

The five committees and their functions are described below:

[2] Reproduced from The 1976 Annual Handbook for Group Facilitators, J. William Pfeiffer and John E. Jones, Editors, University Associates Publishers, Inc. (La Jolla, California, 1976), pp. 15–17.

162 *Fundamentals of Effective Group Communication*

1. Social Activities—develop activities to bring together participants and guests with an emphasis on fun and enjoyment.
2. Intellectual Activities—stimulate an interest in learning and knowledge by having exhibits, demonstrations, discussions, etc., with an emphasis on discovery.
3. Public Relations—publicize information regarding the event as well as report on its progress and conclusion via the news media.
4. Food and Housing—prepare a menu, including refreshments, and provide for rooms and meals for invited guests.
5. Finances—plan a budget and distribute money, sell admission tickets, record expenditures, and prepare a financial report.

You must choose five chairmen from the descriptions of volunteers provided on the Leadership Characteristics Volunteers Description Sheet that follows.

Committee	Individual Choice	Group Choice
1. Social Activities		
2. Intellectual Activities		
3. Public Relations		
4. Food and Housing		
5. Finances		

Leadership Characteristics Volunteers Description Sheet

Jim is an army veteran with combat experience in Vietnam. Although he is somewhat cold and impersonal, he is excellent at organizing and planning. This past term he was largely responsible for the success of a community "Blood Donor Day."

Bob is an outstanding athlete and popular with females. Baseball has been his only activity the past few years. He is a perfectionist, however, and is easily frustrated when working with people.

Frank is a political activist. He seems to be continually involved in some cause or demonstration. He has proven leadership qualities and organized a successful supermarket boycott in the community.

Mary is a very attractive, popular woman who has participated in a number of beauty pageants. She has not been involved in any "task-oriented" activities except for helping to decorate the country club summer dance after being chosen queen.

Jerry is rather shy and withdrawn; his volunteering was a sur-

Leadership–Followership: A Competency Approach

prise. It is rumored that Jerry is seeing a psychiatrist on a weekly basis. The leadership position could be very therapeutic.

Marcia is quite outspoken and at times obnoxious. She usually volunteers for many activities, but she is rarely chosen. She is, however, a very diligent and persistent worker.

Joan did an excellent job in a leadership position for one of the political parties during the past elections. Her political views conflict with Frank's, and they have frequent arguments. She is currently experiencing some marital difficulties, and there are rumors of a possible divorce.

Sue is active with a local dramatic club. She was co-chairman of a community art show which was well received but sparsely attended. However, she and Mary are dating the same young man and presently are not speaking to each other.

John is engaged in a few social organizations and does an adequate job. He is somewhat hypersensitive and prefers to do things himself instead of delegating. As a result, lateness is one of his consistent characteristics.

Adam had a major part in the establishment of a local service organization. He is outgoing and enjoys his social life. During the past year, however, he has been arrested twice on charges of disorderly conduct.

Margie is a pert, smiling individual, who is quite popular with men and never lacks a date. She is not very popular with her female co-workers.

Anne is already over-involved in activities, but she volunteered because she felt she was needed. She has done public relations work for past events and can do an excellent job if she can find enough time.

We believe that the development of a competency direction for leadership depends on evaluating behavior in group situations and modifying those behaviors in order to achieve group effectiveness. We caution you to avoid the supposition that a specific kind of leadership behavior will work in related kinds of group situations. The research simply does not prescribe leader-to-situation traits and behaviors. We believe that you are better advised to learn the group's needs in any given situation and then mix and match group-centered and task-centered behaviors as you try to work for your group.

The major difficulty encountered by students of group discussion methods and leadership training is that the bulk of the research centers around the characteristics of activities that one should learn to perform effectively in a group setting. Therein lies the major difficulty in establishing guidelines for competency for the group process; i.e., group cohesiveness can be developed and measured, but how do you, the student in a classroom setting, deal with your desire and efforts to become prominent in the group situation? You can easily get in the bind of assessing your own individual participation and that of the others in your group and miss the more important behaviors necessary to promote group effectiveness.

We have stressed the important research results that describe rather than prescribe how to emphasize competency in group procedure, group interaction, group functional roles, and membership participation. We believe that you can assess your personal involvement in affecting leadership within your group if you move away from self-centered behaviors that enhance your position and move toward the behaviors that we have emphasized in this chapter.

The perpetual problem of how to measure for competency in any communication process, including group communication and leadership abilities, remains unanswered. But, we do know that the acquisition of the behaviors discussed, outlined, and tested in this chapter may well provide the best path to dealing with leaders and followers as they work together.

Summary

In this chapter we have stressed that leadership is comprised of verbal and nonverbal behaviors that facilitate the achievement of group goals. Towards that end, every group member exhibits greater or lesser amounts of leadership behavior.

An "emergent" leader is preferred in the classroom situation because he or she usually exhibits communicative behaviors that speed the accomplishment of the group's task. We also noted that the emergent leader skilled in human relations and similar communicative behaviors toward the other group members produces a high degree of member satisfaction in his or her leadership. The best evidence to date suggests that a group appears to select as leader a member who creates the expectation that he or she will help the group solve its problem and ensure the groups cohesiveness.

We outlined the research on leader behavior and its relationship to group productivity, cohesiveness, and satisfaction. We then provided a group simulation experience, "Leadership Characteristics," to actualize the material presented in the chapter.

Finally, we encourage you to be sensitive to the pressure to be self-centered rather than group-centered as you communicate your leadership behavior in the group.

References and Further Reading

GOURAN, DENNIS S. "Perspectives on the Study of Leadership: Its Present and Its Future," New Books in Review, in *Quarterly Journal of Speech, 60:* 3 (October, 1974), p. 378.

STOGDILL, RALPH M. *Handbook of Leadership: A Survey of Theory and Research.* New York: The Free Press, 1974, pp. 320–321, 416–417, 422, 428.

WEINBERG, SANFORD B., LARRY J. SMOTROFF, and JOHN C. PECKA. "Communication Factors of Group Leadership," *Journal of Applied Communication Research* (November) 1978, pp. 88–89, 91.

Evaluation/Assessment Systems for Group Discussion

OBJECTIVES:

After studying this chapter, you should be better able to:

Appreciate the role of evaluation/assessment in group discussion.

Understand the concept of formative evaluation.

Understand the concept of summative evaluation.

Engage in critical self-evaluation following participation in a group discussion.

Synthesize individual evaluations and relate the individual evaluations to a group evaluation.

Participate in keeping detailed evaluation records.

FUNDAMENTALS OF GROUP COMMUNICATION[1]

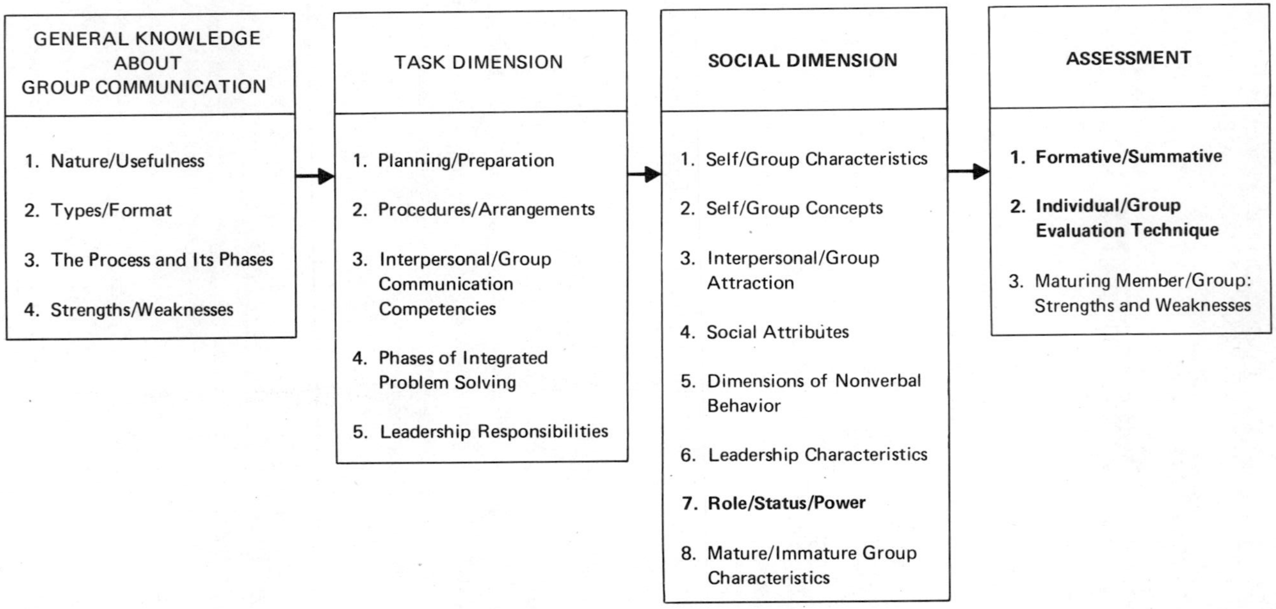

GENERAL KNOWLEDGE ABOUT GROUP COMMUNICATION

1. Nature/Usefulness
2. Types/Format
3. The Process and Its Phases
4. Strengths/Weaknesses

→

TASK DIMENSION

1. Planning/Preparation
2. Procedures/Arrangements
3. Interpersonal/Group Communication Competencies
4. Phases of Integrated Problem Solving
5. Leadership Responsibilities

→

SOCIAL DIMENSION

1. Self/Group Characteristics
2. Self/Group Concepts
3. Interpersonal/Group Attraction
4. Social Attributes
5. Dimensions of Nonverbal Behavior
6. Leadership Characteristics
7. **Role/Status/Power**
8. Mature/Immature Group Characteristics

→

ASSESSMENT

1. **Formative/Summative**
2. **Individual/Group Evaluation Technique**
3. Maturing Member/Group: Strengths and Weaknesses

[1] Concepts in bold face are emphasized in this chapter.

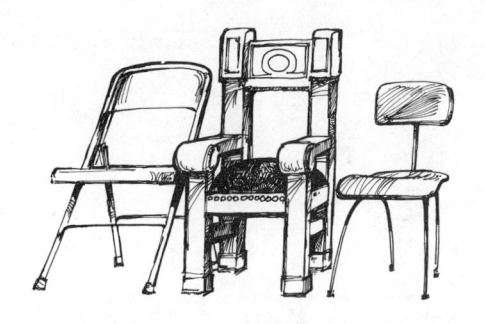

The preceding chapters have dealt with the various theoretical and practical concerns of small-group communication. Earlier chapters have also provided you with the process elements of small groups. The purpose of this chapter is to assist you with concepts to use in evaluating the success of small-group communication. The approach taken in this chapter will enable you to evaluate various independent aspects of the small group communication process and you also will be given information to use in making an overall evaluation.

Formative/Summative Evaluation

An evaluation system has both *formative* and *summative* components. Formative evaluation occurs in the process itself as a participant continually examines the process of communication to determine if the process is being maintained and the participant continually monitors the qualitative aspects of each phase of the discussion. Summative evaluation occurs at the conclusion of the discussion when the entire discussion can be viewed as a whole and from the perspective of the completed task (see Fig. 7-1).

The proverb "Hindsight is better than foresight" emphasizes summative judgment and evaluation, but it is also of tremendous value for an individual participant to engage in formative evaluation. When the participant is continually monitoring the success of each phase of the process, the possibility of total success for the whole discussion increases considerably, and the probability of a much more positive summative evaluation is enhanced.

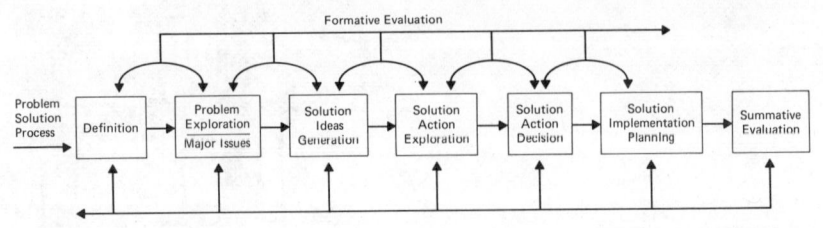

FIGURE 7-1. Model of Formative/Summative Evaluation Applied to Problem-Solution Process.

Because formative evaluation occurs while the process is going on, it provides the advantage of immediate feedback, which allows the group or individual discussant to make internal adjustments in the process. Feedback entails a review of what has just occurred in the discussion, and based on that evaluation reaction, a participant can apply what has been gained (from feedback) to the portion of the discussion yet to come through a feed-forward process, thus improving performance. This constant awareness of evaluating the discussion while it is in progress produces an improved product.

Summative evaluation does not have the advantage of immediate application of the analysis to improve the process. Summative evaluation instead analyzes the product and is an attempt to learn from past experience so that the knowledge can be applied to future experiences.

Evaluating the Individual Participant

Evaluating the group as a whole may not be as productive for you in your own learning process as the individual evaluation of your own participation in the group process. Thus, let us focus on evaluating individual contributions to the group discussion.

Torrance (1953) found that structured evaluation by an expert is the critique process that most effectively brings about the greatest amount of improvement in discussion participants. Structured evaluations by nonexpert peers is the next most suc-

Evaluation/Assessment Systems for Group Discussion

cessful method, followed closely by self-evaluation. Subjects receiving unstructured peer evaluation or no critique at all showed minimal improvement. Thus, you are encouraged to follow carefully the critique and advice of your instructor in order to obtain maximum improvement in your group communication skills. Also, you should contribute your own evaluation of your peers and you should be sensitive to your peers' evaluations of your own participation. Finally, you should engage in self-evaluation as it can help you improve your skill in group communication.

Figure 7-2 contains an individual discussion participant evaluation form that may be used to assess each individual participant in the group. This form provides a framework for an evaluator to make a summative evaluation of each specific individual participating in a group discussion. The categories identified on the form have been treated in preceding chapters. Each of the major evaluation areas of this individual discussion participant evaluation form is briefly reviewed in the succeeding pages.

Research/Preparation

Occasionally, members of small groups are requested to submit briefing material that each member has developed prior to the discussion. This material may then be circulated to other members of the group so that each group member has some understanding of the background of information and knowledge the other members of the group will present. When this is the case, evaluation of an individual's research/preparation can be made directly from the materials submitted.

However, more frequently, individual participants do not submit written material or share the written evidence of their research and preparation. When this is the case, the evaluator must rely on subjective determination of the extent of research and preparation of the individual participant. Additionally, the evaluator must be very alert to the oral contributions made by the individual participant in the discussion when information, facts, statistics, quotations, or other related research material are shared with other members of the group.

Normally, the evaluation of research and preparation can

Name _____

Group Grade _____ Individual grade _____

		Excellent		Average		Poor
1. RESEARCH/PREPARATION — amount — quality	(circle one)	1	2	3	4	5
2. QUANTITATIVE PARTICIPATION — number of comments — length of comments	(circle one)	1	2	3	4	5
3. QUALITATIVE PARTICIPATION — strength of comments — relation of comments to others	(circle one)	1	2	3	4	5
4. ROLE/STATUS — role, understanding and projection — status equalization	(circle one)	1	2	3	4	5
5. OPEN/CLOSED ATTRIBUTES — attitude of openness — risk/threat factors	(circle one)	1	2	3	4	5
6. LEADERSHIP/FOLLOWERSHIP — participation in leadership functions — participation as follower	(circle one)	1	2	3	4	5
7. MAINTENANCE OF THE PROCESS	(circle one)	1	2	3	4	5
8. OVERALL COMMENTS	(circle one)	1	2	3	4	5

FIGURE 7-2. Small Group Communication Individual Participant Evaluation Form.

be based on two main factors: first, the amount of material that an individual participant seems to have developed in preparation for the discussion activity; second, the quality of the information obtained through research and the manner in which it was shared with other members of the group. Quality is usually assessed by the strength of the researched material and the relevance of the research material to the specific issues dealt with in the discussion group.

Quantitative Participation

An untrained evaluator will often place excessive emphasis on the quantity of participation of an individual in assessing that individual's contribution to the group. The untrained evaluator often feels that the person who talks the most must be the person in the group doing the best job of discussion. However, quantity does not equal quality and the trained evaluator will not be fooled by a lot of talk. Too much talk may dominate the discussion and may be a significant negative point of evaluation.

The number of comments that an individual participant makes in a discussion is important, however, and any comprehensive summative evaluation should have an indication of the number of times that each individual participant did contribute orally to the discussion. A good way to obtain this information is to have an individual observer keep a quantitative analysis chart during the course of the discussion. The quantitative analysis chart is shown as Figure 7-3.

Also important in evaluating the quantitative participation of individual group members is the length of time consumed by each comment. Participants are encouraged to seek to generate bliplike interaction in a discussion; short and succinct comments are preferred to long, rambling comments that almost become self-contained mini-speeches. Bliplike comments emphasize the interrelationship among the individual members of a group, and they keep the discussion from being dominated by individual participants who speak often and for long periods at a time.

To assist you in evaluating the length of time that an individual speaks when a participant makes a comment in a group discussion, you may find the blip chart helpful. The blip chart is shown in Figure 7-4.

Qualitative Participation

To evaluate the qualitative participation of an individual member in a group, there are two key areas to consider: first, the

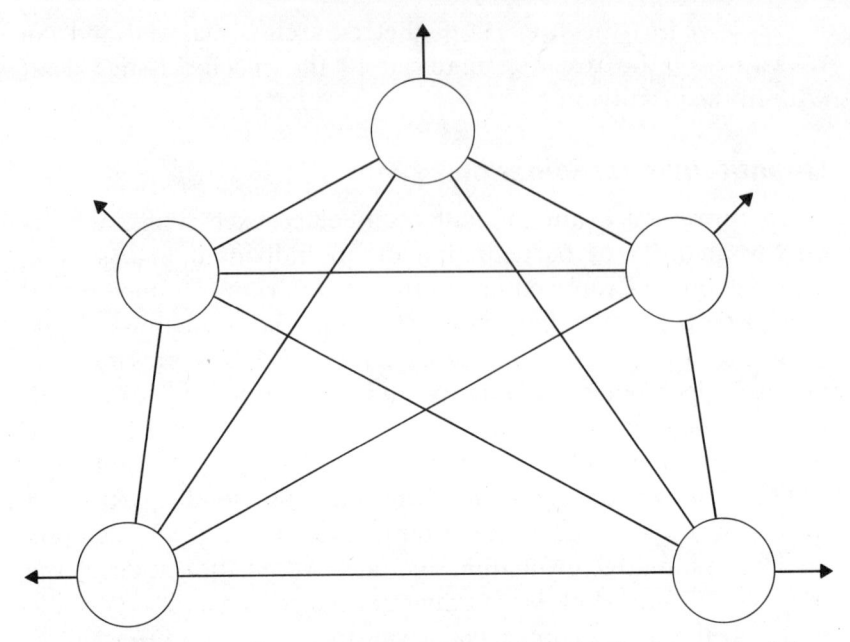

INSTRUCTIONS: Each circle represents a discussion participant. The lines between the circles represent all possible communication links. The short lines pointing away from the group of circles represent a communication link directed to the group at large rather than any specific participant. Each time a participant speaks in a discussion, put an arrow point (>) on the line which shows the direction of the communication. At the conclusion of the discussion, total the arrow points made by each participant in each direction. This will give you the total quantitative participation of each member of the group.

FIGURE 7-3. Quantitative Interaction Analysis Chart.

strength of the comments as related to the overall discussion topic or the specific point in the discussion process; second, the manner in which the individual participant relates each specific point to the preceding comment. Since it is desirable to have the discussion comments flow, it is important that a qualitative evaluation be made of the comments of each discussion participant as they relate to the overall discussion and the immediately preceding comment.

To assist you in making qualitative participation decisions, use the qualitative interaction analysis chart that is shown as Figure 7-5. This provides some further definition and breakdown of the qualitative judgment.

Evaluation/Assessment Systems for Group Discussion 175

	Name		Name
Discussant A	_____	Discussant D	_____
Discussant B	_____	Discussant E	_____
Discussant C	_____	Discussant F	_____

Individual Speaker	2	4	6	8	10	12	S 14	E 16	C 18	O 20	N 22	D 24	S 26	28	30	32	34	36	38	40
1.																				
2.																				
3.																				
4.																				
5.																				
6.																				
7.																				
8.																				
9.																				
10.																				
11.																				
12.																				
13.																				
14.																				
15.																				
16.																				
17.																				
18.																				
19.																				
20.																				

INSTRUCTIONS: Write in identification of each participant so that you can refer to each by the letter referent. As each new speaker in a discussion participates, write the letter referent for that speaker in the first column and then draw out a pencil line to the total number of seconds the individual spoke in that one exchange. Each participant should be listed on a new line each time the participant speaks. You will need several of these sheets for each discussion group session. When the form is completed you will have a bar-graph showing the flow of the discussion by the length of each participation.

FIGURE 7-4. Blip Chart.

176   *Fundamentals of Effective Group Communication*

Group _____

Categories of Analysis	Participant #1	Participant #2	Participant #3	Participant #4	Participant #5	Participant #6	Participant #7	Group TOTAL
shows solidarity								
shows tension release								
agrees								
gives suggestion								
gives opinion								
gives orientation								
asks for orientation								
asks for opinion								
asks for suggestion								
disagrees								
shows tension								
shows antagonism								
Individual TOTALS								

*Adopted from Bales' Interaction Process Analysis

INSTRUCTIONS: Identify the group and then identify each participant by a number from 1 to 7. Each time a participant speaks in the discussion, evaluate the quality of the comment as fitting one of the categories of analysis. Place a line mark (1) in the appropriate box for the participant. At the conclusion of the discussion, total the group and individual columns.

FIGURE 7-5.   Qualitative Interaction Analysis Chart.

Role/Status

This requires a subjective judgment concerning the manner with which an individual participant accepts the role of a group participant and projects into the discussion the role of equal participant. Parallel to a consideration of the role of an individual participant is the matter of the participant's power or status, the level of esteem as assessed by peers. A discussion participant should seek to maintain relatively equal power distribution with other participants throughout the discussion for optimum success of the group. To assist you in evaluating the

Evaluation/Assessment Systems for Group Discussion 177

power/status of individual participants in a group, use the individual member power/status chart shown as Figure 7-6.

Open/Closed Attributes

Judging individual participants in this category requires that the evaluator be a very sensitive observer of these attributes throughout the discussion. There are basically two elements that should be evaluated in this category: first, the extent to which the participant shows a feeling of openness toward all members of the group and toward all topics brought up for discussion; second, the extent to which the individual takes significant risks in the discussion or engages in behavior that might create threat feelings in other members of the group.

Although there is no specific chart designed to assist you in evaluating this category, you might find the qualitative interaction analysis chart somewhat helpful in assessing this area. Several of the categories of analysis on that form relate to the area of open/closed attributes.

Leadership/Followership

Every member of a group demonstrates aspects of leadership or followership and thus should be evaluated in relation to the extent to which each individual served a leadership role or a followership role. To assist you in making this evaluation, use the leadership/followership form that is shown as Figure 7-7. Although this form is designed for group evaluation, it can be used for self-analysis by an individual following the completion of a discussion group. Simply consider how you as an individual would appraise your own participation by using the criteria and scale provided on this form.

Maintenance of the Process

Individual group members need to be careful throughout the discussion to maintain the process. The individual participant must be concerned with this in terms of formative evaluation but it is also a crucial factor in making a summative evaluation

Participant being evaluated _____

Very High Status / Very High Power
Moderately High Status / Moderately High Power
Medium Status / Medium Power
Moderately Low Status / Moderately Low Power
Very Low Status / Very Low Power

Columns (left to right): Beginning of Discussion, 5 Minutes into Discussion, 10 Minutes into Discussion, 15 Minutes into Discussion, 20 Minutes into Discussion, 25 Minutes into Discussion, 30 Minutes into Discussion, 35 Minutes into Discussion, 40 Minutes into Discussion, 45 Minutes into Discussion, 50 Minutes into Discussion, 55 Minutes into Discussion, 60 Minutes into Discussion.

INSTRUCTIONS: Fill in the name of the participant being evaluated. At the beginning of the discussion and at each five minute time interval, place a mark in the column which approximates your evaluation of the participant's power/status from very high to very low. At the conclusion of the discussion, connect the mark in each column with straight lines and you will have a line graph depicting one participant's power/status.

FIGURE 7-6. Individual Member Power/Status Chart.

Evaluation/Assessment Systems for Group Discussion

Group _____

Evaluative Criteria— Leadership Responsibilities	Group Leadership to Single Leader Scale				
	Responsibility Accomplished by Various Group Members				Responsibility Accomplished by Single Leader
1. Introductory Procedures	1	2	3	4	5
2. Preservation of process sequence order	1	2	3	4	5
3. Encouragement of all participants to contribute	1	2	3	4	5
4. Keeping the group on time	1	2	3	4	5
5. Discouraging/calming over-zealous participants	1	2	3	4	5
6. Avoiding/minimizing tangents	1	2	3	4	5
7. Clarifying/restating ambiguous points	1	2	3	4	5
8. Providing transitions	1	2	3	4	5
9. Providing internal summaries	1	2	3	4	5
10. Summation Procedures	1	2	3	4	5

INSTRUCTIONS: Identify the group being evaluated. For each evaluative criteria, make a judgment as to the extent to which that leadership responsibility was fulfilled by various members of the group or by one particular leader-type member. Using the group leadership to single leader scale, circle a number on the scale which reflects your appraisal of how each leadership responsibility was fulfilled.

FIGURE 7-7. Leadership/Followership Form.

of the group. Although much is dependent on the group as a whole as to whether or not all elements of the process are executed, individual members have a responsibility to contribute to the maintenance of the process. It is important for the evaluator to keep the model in mind and to simply check off when each phase of the process has been treated. The form provided in Figure 7-8 will assist you.

Overall Comments

Evaluation should provide the opportunity for general comments. Also, frequently discussions are evaluated in a large

180   Fundamentals of Effective Group Communication

Group _____

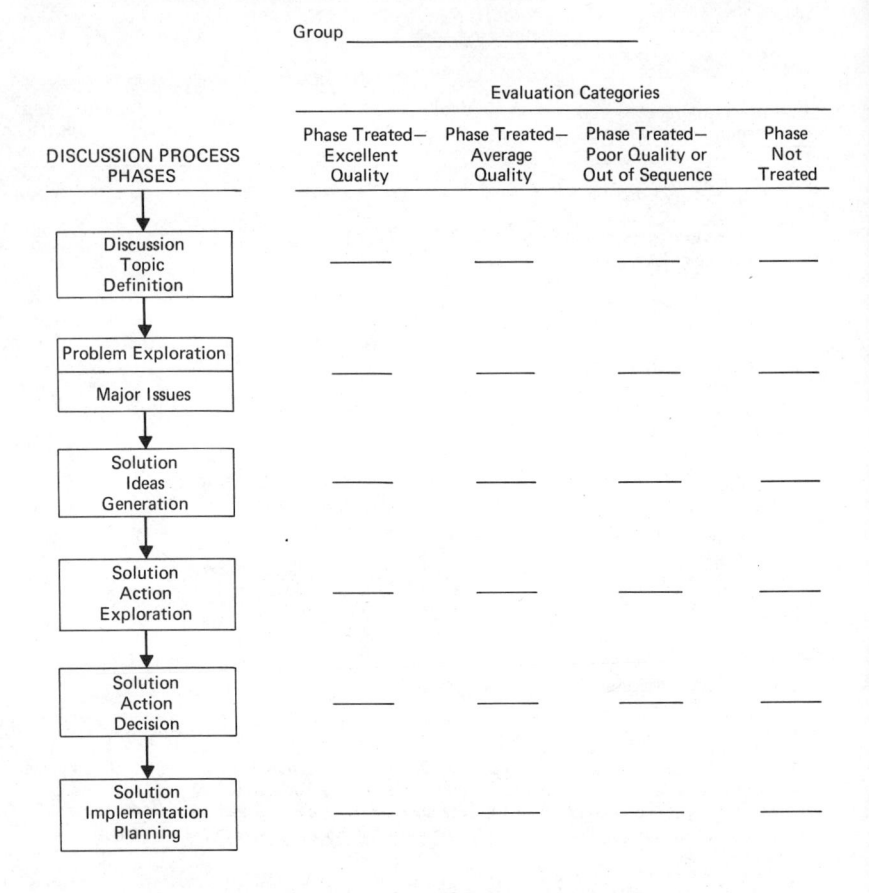

DISCUSSION PROCESS PHASES	Evaluation Categories				
	Phase Treated— Excellent Quality	Phase Treated— Average Quality	Phase Treated— Poor Quality or Out of Sequence	Phase Not Treated
Discussion Topic Definition	_____	_____	_____	_____
Problem Exploration / Major Issues	_____	_____	_____	_____
Solution Ideas Generation	_____	_____	_____	_____
Solution Action Exploration	_____	_____	_____	_____
Solution Action Decision	_____	_____	_____	_____
Solution Implementation Planning	_____	_____	_____	_____

INSTRUCTIONS: Identify the group being evaluated. At the appropriate time in the discussion when each phase should be treated in its proper sequence, place a check (√) in the appropriate space for each phase under evaluation categories.

FIGURE 7-8.   Discussion Process Checklist.

context as to their effectiveness. This section of the evaluation form makes possible general comments on any phase or a broad overall evaluation statement.

Two additional instruments that should be considered for use in making overall comments are the questionnaire for discussion audiences (Fig. 7-9) and group member satisfaction form (Fig. 7-10). The questionnaire for discussion audiences will help individual audience members who are nonparticipants in the discussion to react to the discussion process as it was observed. The

Evaluation/Assessment Systems for Group Discussion

Group _____

INSTRUCTIONS: Answer questions 1–4 by placing a check (√) on the scale at the point which most closely reflects your answer. On Item 5, simply complete the graph.

1. To what extent do you agree with the conclusions of the discussion group?

   |⎯⎯⎯⎯⎯⎯⎯⎯|⎯⎯⎯⎯⎯⎯⎯⎯|⎯⎯⎯⎯⎯⎯⎯⎯|⎯⎯⎯⎯⎯⎯⎯⎯|
   Completely   Completely
   Agree   Disagree

2. To what extent did the group influence you in regard to the questions being discussed?

   |⎯⎯⎯⎯⎯⎯⎯⎯|⎯⎯⎯⎯⎯⎯⎯⎯|⎯⎯⎯⎯⎯⎯⎯⎯|⎯⎯⎯⎯⎯⎯⎯⎯|
   Very   No   Very
   Positively   Influence   Negatively

3. How effectively did the group increase your understanding of the matter under discussion?

   |⎯⎯⎯⎯⎯⎯⎯⎯|⎯⎯⎯⎯⎯⎯⎯⎯|⎯⎯⎯⎯⎯⎯⎯⎯|⎯⎯⎯⎯⎯⎯⎯⎯|
   Great   No
   Increase   Increase

4. Was listening to this discussion a worthwhile activity for you?

   |⎯⎯⎯⎯⎯⎯⎯⎯|⎯⎯⎯⎯⎯⎯⎯⎯|⎯⎯⎯⎯⎯⎯⎯⎯|⎯⎯⎯⎯⎯⎯⎯⎯|
   Great   No
   Worth   Worth

5. Graph the group discussion in progress according to standards learned in this class.

   MINUTES
   GOOD   5   10   15   20   25   30 GOOD

   POOR   POOR

FIGURE 7-9. Questionnaire for Discussion Audiences.

group member satisfaction form encourages the participant in the small-group discussion to react to the group and the process with hindsight feelings following the conclusion of the discussion.

		Definitely Yes				Definitely Not
1.	Did you feel that your group effectively defined its purpose?	1	2	3	4	5
2.	How efficiently did you feel that your group progressed toward the accomplishment of its task?	1	2	3	4	5
3.	Did you feel comfortable and at eash with your group?	1	2	3	4	5
4.	Were you able to express yourself fully and freely in your group?	1	2	3	4	5
5.	Did you feel that your group had effective leadership?	1	2	3	4	5
6.	Did all members of your group participate reasonably equally in the discussion?	1	2	3	4	5
7.	Did you feel that all members of your group made significant contributions to the group's work?	1	2	3	4	5
8.	Did any member of your group attempt to dominate the group process?	1	2	3	4	5
9.	Were all members of your group well prepared for the discussion?	1	2	3	4	5
10.	Did your group maintain the process of an effective discussion group?	1	2	3	4	5

Total your score

10 – 20 You think the discussion generally went well and you generally have good feelings about your group.

20 – 30 You think the discussion generally went okay and you are reasonably pleased with your group.

30 – 40 You think this discussion didn't go well and you don't have very good feelings about your group.

40 – 50 You think this discussion was awful and you have very negative feelings about your group.

FIGURE 7-10. Group Member Satisfaction Form.

Summary

This chapter defined and explained formative and summative evaluation. It presented an overall evaluation chart for use in the assessment of individual performance in a group discussion and described in detail each phase of this form. It included also numerous other forms designed to assist the evaluator in performing a comprehensive assessment of individual and group performance in discussion.

References and Further Reading

BRADEN, WALDO W., and EARNEST BRANDENBURG. *Oral Decision-Making.* New York: Harper & Row, 1955, Ch. 16.

BRANDENBURG, ERNEST, and PHILIP A. NEAL, "Graphic Techniques for Evaluating Discussion and Conference Procedures," *Quarterly Journal of Speech,* 39 (1953), pp. 201–8.

CROWELL, LAURA, "Rating Scales as Diagnostic Instruments in Discussion," *The Speech Teacher,* 2 (1953), pp. 26–32.

GULLEY, HALBERT E., *Discussion, Conference, and Group Process* (2nd Ed.). New York: Holt, Rinehart and Winston, 1968, Ch. 16.

HOWELL, WILLIAM S., and DONALD K. SMITH. *Discussion, Part IV.* New York: Macmillan, 1956.

KELTNER, JOHN W., *Group Discussion Processes.* New York: David McKay, Ch. 24.

SMITH, WILLIAM S., *Group Problem Solving Through Discussion.* Indianapolis: Bobbs-Merrill, 1965, Ch. 9.

THOMPSON, WAYNE N., "A Study of Factors Considered by Students in Evaluating Public Discussions," *Speech Monographs,* 20 (1953), pp. 268–72.

TORRANCE, E. PAUL, "Methods of Conducting Critiques of Group Problem-Solving Performance," in Hare, A. Paul, Borgatta, E. F., and Bales, R. F., *Small Groups: Studies in Social Interaction* (rev. ed.). New York: Alfred A. Knopf, 1966, pp. 692–9.

When Groups "Go Good or Bad": Effective Strategies

OBJECTIVES:

After reading this chapter, you should be able to:

Identify and describe the essential elements of a "mature" group.

Identify and describe the behaviors of "immature" members and groups and the effective strategies to move toward a maturing group experience.

Identify and describe the characteristics of a functioning "mature" group.

Appreciate and utilize the necessary factors of adjusting and growing as a member and as a group.

FUNDAMENTALS OF GROUP COMMUNICATION[1]

GENERAL KNOWLEDGE ABOUT GROUP COMMUNICATION

1. Nature/Usefulness
2. Types/Format
3. The Process and Its Phases
4. Strengths/Weaknesses

TASK DIMENSION

1. Planning/Preparation
2. Procedures/Arrangements
3. Interpersonal/Group Communication Competencies
4. Phases of Integrated Problem Solving
5. Leadership Responsibilities

SOCIAL DIMENSION

1. Self/Group Characteristics
2. Self/Group Concepts
3. Interpersonal/Group Attraction
4. Social Attributes
5. Dimensions of Nonverbal Behavior
6. Leadership Characteristics
7. Role/Status/Power
8. **Mature/Immature Group Characteristics**

ASSESSMENT

1. Formative/Summative
2. Individual/Group Evaluation Technique
3. **Maturing Member/Group: Strengths and Weaknesses**

[1] Concepts in bold face are emphasized in this chapter.

The life and times of a group, i.e., your classroom situations, campus groups, and everyday contacts with family and friends, are initiated and held together by the communication abilities of each member. Quite simply, it is through communication and only by that process that a group is called a group.

Theoretically, we have stressed that you need to be aware of how communication works and how you can have a high degree of influence and control over how communication works in a group. We have argued the case for a knowledge of theory and an understanding of how theory works in practice throughout the preceding chapters. We are particularly interested in your learned ability to locate and isolate potential communication problem in your group, and to work toward the eventual resolution of those difficulties. Knowing (theory) and doing (practice) need not be two different processes.

In this chapter, we are going to examine the life-cycle problems of student groups when they either go "sour" and/or "spoil" or when they go "sour" and become "good" and somehow stay fresh and capable of maturation.

When Groups "Go Good"

We have found the metaphor of "immature–mature" to be a useful means of dealing with the life and growth of a group, even one of such short-term duration as is found in the classroom. We believe that the essential elements of a group, mature in its theoretical and practical awareness of group communication skills, are the following:

1. *There is a growth rather than a loss of self-hood in the group.* Contrary to what you might think, there need not be a "group-think" phobia operating in groups whereby all participants think and act as one. Groups that work and grow together should and often do promote the multiplication of "selves" within each member prepared to meet and deal with the varied personalities of a group. A mature group member and and a mature group exhibit an expansive sense of high self-concept and group communication skills that match their confidence in themselves.
2. *The mature group exists in an atmosphere of trust and friendship.* Mature group members support what they help to create; they tend to encourage and effect sound group decisions when they share equally in the discussion; and they tend to generate constructive follow-up action when they share the same goals and aspirations for success.
3. *The mature group shows a uniform concern, a positive regard for the least, the loudest, and the best of its members.* No one in the maturing group gets special attention or undue preference for their good or not-so-good ideas. So many groups, if research is to be our sole guide, suffer from a consistent pattern of acceptance and rejection of people and their ideas because of past successes or failures in discussion situations. The maturing groups learn, through much pain and struggle, to weigh ideas and personalities in terms of their *value* and not according to *who* expressed them. These interpersonal and group-centered lessons are so hard to learn, but are so valuable to acquire.
4. *The mature group uses positive nonverbal communication to help each member to participate, to struggle with issues, personalities, and with themselves.* In our earlier chapter on nonverbal communication we stressed the importance of using nonverbal cues to show your involvement in and concentration on the discussion. We have found a consistent thread of intensity in the body stance, the facial expressions, the gestures, and the overall supportive nature of an involved group member. A careful study of your nonverbal behaviors and the constructive methods we have suggested will help you become a mature member of your group.

5. *The mature group strains; it adapts to points of disagreement.* The maturing group searches for points of agreement at every opportunity but more important, it eagerly and actively prepares itself for disagreement. Time after time the business of group problem solving is centered in conflict and crisis-type communication. Maturing groups exploit their creative energies, their sense of when to use persuasive communication, and their openness to maximize the frustrations, anger, and misunderstanding in order to "fight through the wall" and come to a consensus agreement. Maturing groups show those special talents necessary to make disagreement and conflict strengthen rather than weaken their togetherness. Immature groups allow crisis and conflict to destroy them. They are incapable of working with and through difficulties to overcome their individual and group weaknesses.
6. *The mature group is marked by members who are ready and willing to relinquish any position in the group for the general benefit of the group.* We have discussed at some length in earlier chapters the establishment and maintenance of role-related behaviors among leaders and followers. There is no conflict with the changing and shifting of roles as suggested here. What is actually at work in this attribute of maturity is the strength of each member's self-concept, a solid degree of self-confidence to do the work required by the group's task without regard for labels, officers, or status. In a real sense, the mature group member can "answer the phone," issue an order, take an order, or perform any other activity that needs to be done. On the other hand, immature members get into and remain locked in comfortable or authoritarian roles, refusing to "soil their hands" with work to be done.
7. *Finally, the mature group has a good time!* In the years that we have been involved with countless student and professional groups, we have been impressed by the mature "work/play" attitude of experienced group members. Maturing group members, each in his or her own way, not only come to grips with an appreciation of the art and science of group discussion, but they also come, again each in his or her own way, to *love* the group experience. It is most difficult for us to explain this most intangible of the behaviors of mature

groups. But, simply stated, there does exist a certain joy of the trials and tribulations of group problem solving and an eagerness to engage in the work/play of group discussion. You can actually experience this feeling. By contrast, immature members see only the work and flee from a real opportunity to feel the joy of working together, laughing together, and looking forward to the next experience together.

Mature or immature groups are entities unto themselves encompassing the numerous dimensions and factors discussed so far. The maturation process for a group can certainly be retarded by the regressive efforts of immature members. We are not trying to create an unnecessary conflict here when we discuss the notion of an immature group *member* and an immature *personality*. Maturity is defined here as a combination of perceived skills and strengths. The immature member is defined as one who for reasons of lack of knowledge about groups, a tacit or open refusal to learn how to improve his or her position in the group, or for any combination of reasons, just does not progress in effective group functioning and group skills.

When Groups "Go Bad"

It is as natural as any aspect of group behavior to have awkward and troublesome times, i.e., members arguing, members "stonewalling," members subverting the group's efforts, and so on. These are facts of group life. If allowed to fester, they infect the entire group. It is also natural for groups to engage in collective behaviors that lead nowhere, express anger, apathy, hostility, boredom, and general confusion. It is important to note that in each situation (problems of individual members and those of groups) there are answers to combat problems and to encourage improvement. There are situations and understandings that you can be competent in as a member of your group when you, your colleagues, or your entire group encounter problems.

When Groups "Go Good or Bad": Effective Strategies 191

1. *In the majority of cases, immature members want to help, but they don't receive the special handling necessary to feel accepted.*

    Sometimes new members tend to hold back on participating and, if allowed, seem to develop reticent communication behaviors. Obviously, any new member of a group might be tense, feeling a low sense of status and an uncertainty about his or her place in the group.

    Rule 1. Be especially sensitive to the "entry" remarks of new members. To help new group members feel accepted, you should respond with nonverbal as well as verbal approval. The likelihood is that the new members will feel accepted. Acceptance is the most important virtue in a group setting where nearly everyone is new to each other. If as time passes their shyness persists, pay attention to the new members outside the discussion, talk with them, learn more about them. To have friends in your group, you need to be a friend sensitive to attempts to enter the group.

    Rule 2. In actual discussion, and before questions and/or requests are directed toward any individual member, the shy, nonparticipating member should be "warned." By encouraging all of the group that everyone is free to participate and that everyone's contributions are the group's property, a sense of "we-ness" and/or cohesion can permeate the atmosphere of discussion. In this manner, no one needs to feel alone in the lack of or excess of involvement because contributions once uttered become the domain of the group to treat and discuss.

    Rule 3. Questions directed to only one member should be framed so that they can be answered with the information available to that individual. It does more harm than good to ask a question that shy members can't answer well. As time goes along, the reticent member will be more at ease, and his or her communication will improve in quality and usefulness to the efforts of the group.

2. *On the other end of the spectrum, an immature member often monopolizes discussion for his or her own ends.*

    Rule 1. There are a variety of strategies to use in such a circumstance. You and your group should be extremely cautious about "slapping the wrists" of a member involved in a role-struggle "war." In such cases, the maturing member/group must "keep cool"; the monopolizer may behave in this manner because the group is partly responsible for the behaviors of all of its members. To that member's credit, he or she may be groping for a desired or needed position in the group. Don't discourage the member's volume of "talk" because it is consuming valuable time. It's everyone's mature task in this setting to weigh the nature of the communication, and if that member is actually wasting precious time, then let the group deal with the whole problem of regulating everyone's communication.

Rule 2. Quite often an overanxious group member really has a great deal to say and wants to "show and tell" everything he or she knows so that the group will like and accept him or her. Sincerity and eagerness to participate are admirable virtues. Yet, you and other members can alter the lengths of "speeches" in discussion by the use of questions, reminders to everyone to focus their remarks, and by gently informing the group that everyone must regulate communication so that each point can be addressed, if desired by everyone. By encouragement and politeness, the overachievers and the underachievers can blend with the middle-of-the road group members to respond to the challenge of becoming better than they are—to become mature members.

3. *Groups "go bad" with more regularity when members are argumentative, hostile, or obstinate.*

Rule 1. More than likely, the vocal, somewhat hostile member is deeply involved in the subject under discussion. This person is not being a "stick in the mud" just to be angry. Rather, he or she is deeply ego involved and therefore highly opinionated about the subject.

You should learn early on in discussion matters that you must not dismiss the person or ideas presented, just because the delivery and nonverbal communication are "out of the ordinary." If your listening skills are ever called into play in a crisis setting, this is it! Listen for evidence and conclusion making. Make sure that you weigh the links between the ideas being expressed, the evidence for them, and the conclusion(s) developed from them. You may find that the angry member is a potentially valuable and contributing member.

Rule 2. Anger is certainly a dangerous behavior because, if unbridled, resulting intragroup hostilities can destroy group effectiveness as quickly as any behavior known to group discussion experiences. *Keep you own temper at any cost* and try to help others maintain their "cool"! You may even have to tell your group *in discussion* to be aware of the detrimental effects of "hot" language on the group's overall task. You may even suggest a recess so that matters can be talked over and feelings allowed to cool down. The group should not move any further in their deliberations until the people and issues in deepest conflict are composed and resolved. Remember, quite often the *best* work of a group may result from an airing of candid feelings and emotions. A mature group gradually develops an expansive atmosphere of trust and openness so that *all* comments can be shared, even those expressions of anger and hostility.

Characteristics of a Functioning Mature Group

1. *There is an equality, a balance of interaction among all members.* Group members find agreement and support for the roles that they assume in a situational balance of task behavior and group maintenance behavior. The maturing group realizes, ever so gradually, that enthusiasm and creativity are the keys to agreement and disagreement. Given its head, the group will find its own level of involvement and systematic coverage of the subject.
2. *There is a comfortable, cooperative atmosphere among all members.* The maturing group becomes acutely aware that there are probably as many ways of making an idea clear as there are people in the group. The sensitive member shows a deep willingness to take the time and effort to choose among the many ways of expression so that cooperation and understanding are the result rather than disharmony and misun-

derstanding. A cooperative group atmosphere is clearly the result of deciding what should *not* be communicated as much as what *should* be communicated.
3. *There is an effective situational brand of leadership that leads to a thorough analysis of data and solutions.* We have stressed earlier that leadership, properly assumed by all members in general and a task-related supervisor in particular, is the key to balancing work and play toward an effective conclusion. Again, remember, consensus or unanimous agreement on the task is the singular goal of the problem-solving group. Shared leadership behaviors are the best time- and research-proven ways by which the mature group achieves its goals.

Summary

In conclusion, it is important to know that group members, like any other communicator-format situation, are capable of adjusting themselves in order to become more effective in their group relationships. Leaders, members, and group situations are all flexible elements in the discussion process, where making choices regarding behaviors are accepted necessities. The maturing group member is constantly controlling him- or herself, his or her communication and membership in the group. Surely, things "go good and bad" in the life of a group.

The differences between the strategies available for the group member to display immaturity or maturity are challenges available to all. You need to decide which road you want to travel toward finding your *self*, your communication skills, and your good sense. Therein lies your path to becoming a mature member of your group.

References and Further Reading

BERNE, ERIC. *Games People Play.* New York: Grove Press, 1964.
GOFFMAN, ERVING W. *The Presentation of Self in Everyday Life.* New York: Doubleday, 1959.

SCHEIDEL, THOMAS M. and CROWELL, LAURA. *Discussing and Deciding: A Desk Book for Group Leaders and Members.* New York: Macmillan Publishing Co., Inc., 1979.

Index

Artifactual Communication, 117
Assigned topics, 43
   subcategory analysis, 43

Communication competencies, 75–80
   competent communicator, 78
   interpersonal, 75
   group, 75
   group-centered core of, 80–81
   list of, 78–80
   testing, lack of, 80
Communication model, 7
Cross-cultural communication, 65–66

Decision-making procedures checklist, 88
Discussion
   purpose of, 35
   types of questions
      fact, 36
      policy, 36–37
      value, 36

Emergent leader
   communication behaviors, 158–59
Evaluation
   formative/summative, 169–70
   evaluating of the individual, 170–71
   quantitative participation, 173–76
   qualitative participation, 173
   overall comments, 179–82
   research/participation, 171–73
   role/status, 177–78

Facial communication, 111–13
   body contact, 115
   eye (gaze), 113–14
   gestures, 114–15
   posture, 115
Feedback, 7–8
Feedforward, 7

Groups
   classroom, difficulty of, 69
   interpersonal attraction, 68
   location of, 38–39
   open/closed attributes, 177
   people-oriented, 33
   process of, 6-9
   psychological drives to join, 62–63
   purposes of, 9
   social dimension, 8–9
   spar of commitment, 68–69
   strengths of, 22–25
   task dimensions, 8–9
   task-oriented, 33
   types
      briefing session, 12–13
      staff meeting, 12
      study group, 12
   uses of, 5–6
   weaknesses of, 25–26

Hidden agenda, 37–38
Human motivation
   list of, 60–62

Ideal discussants, 33
Information,
   clarity of, 47
   concise records, 46–47
   consistency of, 49–50
   recency of, 49
   record, 47
   source credibility, 48–49
   statement of fact or opinion, 48
   statistical, 50–51
      accuracy of, 51–52
   thoroughness of, 50
Immature-mature group, 187–93
   strategies for, 190–93
Interaction process analysis, 88–89
Interpersonal communication competencies
   list of, 76–77
Interpersonal communication, 77

197

Kinesics, 111

Leader behavior
  related to group productivity, 160–61
Leadership
  characteristics situation description sheet, 161–62
  characteristics volunteers description sheet, 162–63
  characteristics worksheet, 155–56
  definition of, 156–57
  directions for competency, 163–64
  emergent leader, 157–58
Leadership/followership, 177
  characteristics of, 193–94
  process maintenance, 177–79

Mature group, 188–90
Motivated behavior, 60

Noise
  in discussion, 42–43
Nonverbal communication
  confident/uncertain, 119–20
  definition, 106
  importance to small groups, 108–10
  importance to society, 108–09
  observing and interpreting, 118–19
  open/closed, 119
  part of language systems, 110–11
  pensive/aggressive, 120–21
  test, 121–45
  test explanation, 146–51
  verbal-nonverbal differences, 106–108

Phases in integrated problem solving, 89–99
  process dimensions
    social, 8–9
    task, 8–9
Proxemic, 115–16
Psychological screens in discussion, 63–68
  external systems, 67

Psychological screens in discussion (cont.)
  internal forces, 67
  interaction potential, 67
  heterophily, 67
  homophily, 67
  perceptual, 65
  semantic, 65

Research
  books, 43
  encyclopedia-type works, 44
  magazines, 44–45
  pamphlets, 45–46
  past experience, 43
  personal contacts, 46

Seating arrangement
  face off, 39
  head man, 40
  look at us, 40–41
  we're all in it together, 41–42
Self-discovery, 59
Small group communication
  appropriate use of, 21
  decision making
    boards, 16–17
    conference, 15–16
    committee/council, 14
    decision making, 13
    task force, 14–15
  definition of, 3–4
  evaluation of, 169
  formats
    closed, 17–18
    dialogue, 19–20
    decision making, 10
    fact finding, 10–11
    forum, 20–21
    hybrid, 21
    information sharing, 10–11
    panel, 20
    symposium, 20
Statistics
  sampling problems, 52
  uses of, 53

Techniques Test, 82–86
  scoring of, 86–88

Vocalized Communication, 117–18